THE·POET'S WORK

THE POET'S WORK

By John Holmes

NEW YORK

OXFORD UNIVERSITY PRESS

1939

Printed in the United States of America

TO

SARA LUDLOW HOLMES

AND

JOHN LUDLOW HOLMES

THIS

AND ALL MY WORK

CONTENTS

FOREWORD

ANYONE who reads this book, the result of a good many years of gathering sentences from other writers for the purpose of making poetry and poets more understandable, will inevitably make two comments. More are possible, but two are certain. They will say that such a book as this one is, after all, a compilation by one man of the best work of scores of better men. And they will suggest, to themselves or to me, excellent passages from excellent writers which ought to have been included.

Discoverers of this book are likely to feel that such a book is dishonourably easy to make. One reads comfortably and pleasantly, one marks or copies interesting passages, and at leisure one patches them together into a book, without having exerted any real creative energy, they think. But those who have attempted such a task have surely wished, as I have wished, that they had set themselves to write the whole thing single-handed rather than carry to completion the endless details of allocating, checking, and getting permission to use the hundreds of quotations which give this book its only real value. The labour of making, arranging, and obtaining rights to use such material is unbelievably complicated, exasperating, and dull. For several years I worked for myself and my own pleasure; for one year I worked for some not impossible readers; and for nearly another year I worked for publishers and agents and the law of copyright. There was small pleasure in the final labour. None of it will be appreciated by the reader. Without it no anthology could exist.

This book began to insist on its right to be a book some ten years before actual publication, although at that time I had not heard its voice. By uncounted degrees, a series of disappointments, hours and days and weeks of back-break and eye-strain I can now hardly believe, the voice became louder, louder, more familiar, until at last it told me what to do. I had the excitement and pleasure and weariness of copying the book from the first page to the last, essays and quotations, five times over, revising, adding, rejecting and correcting with each new manuscript. And now that it exists in type and pages and cover I realize that it is the end of a certain chapter in my life. I have used to some advantage my interest in what artists have said about the life of the artist, and I must move on to other matters, other books, later chapters of experience.

This concentration, this nucleus, this repository of the wisdom artists have written down is capable of infinite extension. No one knows that better than I do, looking ruefully at the pages of excised poems, journals, letters, essays and other material on my work-table.

There are books I have not so much as heard of, not to speak of having examined and weighed for the purposes of this book. There are whole systems of aesthetic theory, of literary criticism, of ascertainable poetic experience, which I have not so much as sampled. But I hope to have suggested, in spite of certain likings and convictions, that they exist and have not been quoted. I am, for instance, acutely aware of the critical essays of Mr. T. S. Eliot, largely unrepresented in this book. His writing is so extremely quotable that one or two extracts must be taken as testament. There are others, less known to the general reader, more enthusiastically urged by the expert. I might have used more of Shakespeare, for did not he say everything worth saying?

I might have exemplified the humanist, the Marxist, the romantic, the classicist more than I did. With equal good reason I might have represented John Donne, John Keats, Edwin Arlington Robinson, Leonardo da Vinci, Vincent Van Gogh, D. H. Lawrence, John Skelton, Robert Herrick, R. P. Blackmur, George Santayana, Goethe, Hopkins, and Rilke and Henry James more fully than I have. What of it? I might also have quoted Emerson, Yeats, Thoreau, and Frost less frequently, and used less of Montaigne and myself. Certainly less of myself. But why? Had anyone else made this book, I would prefer it to have a bias, and the colour that comes of it, rather than a round representation of all literatures and tastes, just, comfortable, and grey.

My immediate hope for this small book is that it will be found by right readers, carried about, urged on more readers, and cared for by them as I have come to care for it, making it. My next hope is that these right readers, or any others, will send suggestions for new and really useful material to me in care of the publishers. My wildest, most distant hope is that this book may be by sufficient demand revised, enlarged and continued as a sort of bible, in small letters, for the young poet who is smart enough to wish to live to be a great poet, for the teachers and prophets who realize that they have the future in their hands, and for critics who have it in their authority and care to guide the literature of their times by the rebuke of bad artists and the praise of good.

One other thing I wish to say. I believe in this book and its power to exhilarate the creative mind. No matter what the effort of construction has been, these pages of great words from the writers of all ages have never failed to lift and enlarge my own vision. I believe they will do the same thing for other readers. Small as the book is, I think it should not be taken in quantity, but eaten of many times, a little at a time. I have tried to print passages that concentrated whole essays, and rhymes that said more than books. I have with a certain perverseness put contradictory passages next one another. Wise teachers may, I think, use this book for the fruitful bewilderment of their students, if both students and teachers are old enough to argue their way forward from bewilderment to conviction. I might have used my material to make a text, combined with usual deadening chapters on versification and poetic strategy. But I have chosen to be of no obvious help to those who have not in themselves the capacity for learning these matters, and all that grows from them. I have chosen with deliberate intention to offer my findings for what they are, and to say little about them, in so far as my several essays say anything. I believe that the student of poetry or of the good life learns most from himself, the teacher being one of many guides or boundary walls against which he must blunder to find the way.

That the way is worth finding I need not insist; but many hours of life devoted to one thing, this book for instance, are not so spent for personal glory or selfish satisfaction. After the unimportant fact of the compiler's care has been realized, after the profoundly important fact of the difficult honour and joy of the artist's life has been perhaps only partially understood, I would hope but for one thing more. I would hope that all who partly know, and some who have not known till now, find in this book a way to a wider and richer life in whatever condition they live it, through knowing the poet's work toward that very end.

My gratitude for assistance in preparing this book is owing more than I can indicate here to my wife; to Richard S. Beal, Harrison M. Hayford, Myron J. Files, Harold H. Blanchard, Charles Gott, and the staff of Eaton Memorial Library, at Tufts College; to Louella D. Everett, Edgar Lee Masters, Theodore Roethke, Ruth Blodgett, Malcolm Cowley, Jessica Nelson North, Ford Madox Ford, John Cournos, E. M. Forster, Robert Frost, Christopher Morley, O. Kenneth Wrigley, Lucien Price, R. P. Blackmur, Max J. Herzberg, Helen Davies McGlade, John

Ciardi, Charles Manning, and Welborn Hope for permission to quote their work, or for the generous loan of valuable books, or for patient answers to my questions; and to the *Atlantic Monthly* for permission to use in a revised form an essay which appeared with the title 'Great Rich Vine.'

Acknowledgement is hereby made to other magazines for permission to reprint verse or prose which first appeared in their pages: to *The Commonweal* for part of a poem by Eileen Duggan; to *Poetry*: *A Magazine of Verse* for a passage from an editorial by Jessica Nelson North; to the *New York Herald-Tribune Books* for some prose by Malcolm Cowley and part of a verse by John Jay Chapman; to *The Nation* for a sentence from an article by Conrad Aiken; and to the *Saturday Review of Literature* for extracts from the writings of Christopher Morley, Archibald MacLeish, William Rose Benét, Arthur Davison Ficke, Henry S. Canby, Frank Jewett Mather, Stella Benson, and Welborn Hope.

Acknowledgement of permission to quote from books is hereby made to Charles Scribner's Sons for extracts taken from *The Middle Years*, by Henry James; *Soliloquies in England*, by George Santayana; *The Enjoyment of Poetry*, by Max Eastman; *Axel's Castle*, by Edmund Wilson; *Tatterdemalion*, by John Galsworthy; *Adventures in Criticism*, by Sir Arthur Quiller-Couch; *Preludes for Memnon* and *Selected Poems*, by Conrad Aiken; *The Wind in the Willows*, by Kenneth Grahame; and *Across the Plains*, by Robert Louis Stevenson.

To the J. B. Lippincott Co., for permission to quote from *Romany Stain, Inward Ho!, John Mistletoe,* and *Human Being,* by Christopher Morley; and from *The Art Spirit,* by Robert Henri.

To Doubleday, Doran & Co., Inc., to Mrs. Rudyard Kipling, and to Messrs. A. P. Watt & Son for permission to quote from *A Book of Words,* by Rudyard Kipling.

To Doubleday, Doran & Co., Inc., for permission to quote from *The Right Place,* by C. E. Montague; *Harriet Hume: a London Fantasy,* by Rebecca West, copyright, 1929; *Notes on My Books,* by Joseph Conrad, copyright, 1920, 1921; *The Nigger of the Narcissus,* by Joseph Conrad, copyright, 1897; *Intellectual Things,* by Stanley Kunitz, copyright, 1929; and *A Writer's Notes on His Trade,* by C. E. Montague.

To Alfred A. Knopf, Inc., for permission to quote from *The Journal of Katherine Mansfield* and *The Letters of Katherine Mansfield; The Hill of Dreams,* by Arthur Machen; *Peter Whiffle,* by Carl Van Vechten; *Prejudices, Third Series,* by H. L. Mencken; and *Two Gentlemen in Bonds,* by John Crowe Ransom.

To the Viking Press, Inc., for permission to quote from *Studies in Classic American Literature,* by D. H. Lawrence, copyright, 1925; *The Letters of D. H. Lawrence,* copyright, 1932; *The Flowering Stone,* by George Dillon, copyright, 1931; *A Portrait of the Artist as a Young Man,* by James Joyce, copyright, 1916; *A Story-Teller's Story,* by Sherwood Anderson, copyright, 1924; and *Blossoming Antlers*, by Winifred Welles, copyright, 1933.

To Random House, Inc., for permission to quote from *Poems* by Stephen Spender; and *Poems* by W. H. Auden.

To Modern Library for permission to quote from William Butler Yeats's introduction to their edition of the poems of William Blake.

To Houghton Mifflin Co., for permission to quote from the essays and journals of Ralph Waldo Emerson; the journals of Henry David Thoreau; *Poems 1924-1933*, by Archibald MacLeish; *Writing Poetry*, by Marie Gilchrist; *The Trusty Knave*, by Eugene Manlove Rhodes; *The Dance of Life*, by Havelock Ellis; *John Keats*, by Amy Lowell; *The Architecture of Humanism*, by Geoffrey Scott; and the journals of John Burroughs.

To G. P. Putnam's Sons, for permission to quote from *The Art of Writing*, by Sir Arthur Quiller-Couch.

To the Condé Nast Publications, Inc., for permission to quote from 'Work and Echo', by Arthur Schnitzler.

To Sheed & Ward, for permission to quote from *Form in Modern Poetry*, by Herbert Read.

To the Caxton Printers, for permission to quote from *Streams From the Source*, by Helene Mullins.

To the G. & C. Merriam Co., for permission to quote from *Word Study* part of an article entitled 'Marlowe's Mighty Line', by Max J. Herzberg.

To W. W. Norton Co., for permission to quote

from *Exile's Return*, by Malcolm Cowley; *The Meaning of Culture*, by John Cowper Powys; *The Notebook of Malte Laurids Brigge*, by Rainer Maria Rilke; and *Discovering Poetry*, by Elizabeth Drew.

To the Bobbs-Merrill Co., for permission to quote from *Everyman's Genius*, by Mary Austin.

To Henry Holt & Co., for permission to quote from *Language*, by Otto Jespersen; *Motley and Other Poems*, by Walter de la Mare; *Address to the Living*, by John Holmes; *A Boy's Will*, *West-Running Brook*, *New Hampshire*, and *A Further Range*, by Robert Frost.

To Farrar & Rinehart, Inc., for permission to quote from *A Draft of XXX Cantos*, by Ezra Pound.

To Harcourt Brace & Co., for permission to quote from *On Reading Shakespeare*, *Afterthoughts*, and *The Prospects of Literature*, by Logan Pearsall Smith; *The Imagination*, by I. A. Richards; *Play in Poetry*, by Louis Untermeyer; *Collected Essays*, by T. S. Eliot; *Abinger Harvest*, by E. M. Forster; *Orlando*, *To the Lighthouse*, and the *Common Reader, First and Second Series*, by Virginia Woolf.

To the Oxford University Press, for permission to quote from *The Letters of Gerard Manley Hopkins to Robert Bridges*, and the *Correspondence of Gerard Manley Hopkins and Richard Watson Dixon*, edited by C. C. Abbott; *The Notebooks and Papers of Gerard Manley Hopkins*, edited by C. C. Abbott; and *Poems*, by Gerard Manley Hopkins.

To the Macmillan Co., for permission to quote from *Strict Joy*, by James Stephens; *Collected*

Poems, by William Butler Yeats; *Essays*, by William Butler Yeats; *Autobiographies*, by William Butler Yeats; *Selected Poems*, by Æ (George Russell); *Collected Poems*, by John Masefield; *A Shakesperian Grammar*, by E. A. Abbott; *Designed for Reading*, edited by H. S. Canby, Christopher Morley, William Rose Benét and Amy Loveman; *Poems*, by Eileen Duggan; and *Letters*, by R. L. Nettleship.

Such laborious acknowledgements clear one's debt to the holders of copyright, which is fair and right; there are other obligations to be discharged, though they are not easy to define. In the first place, I am painfully aware that, though I have been at some pains to thank both persons incorporated and persons as yet private and alive, I have by no means recalled and thanked the friends, students, writers, enemies, rivals, relations, critics, publishers, and people at large who are always helping to make a book whether they know it or not. My thanks are hereby extended to them.

But not all this is enough. In the prefatory mood (which is of course not at all prefatory but backward-gazing) I should like to summon from their exaltation the spirits of Ralph Waldo Emerson, and Henry David Thoreau, and Gerard Manley Hopkins, and Thomas Carlyle, and John Donne to thank them for having written what they wrote. They had more books in them than they published, and mine is least among them. I am glad for the industry and curiosity of Samuel Taylor Coleridge; the heartiness of William Hazlitt; the visions of William Blake, and Walt Whitman, and Thomas Traherne, who said, 'You never enjoy the world aright, till the Sea itself floweth in your veins, till you are clothed with the heavens, and crowned with the stars.' What would these be without the warmth and light of John Keats, without the shrewdness of Montaigne, Jonson, Schopenhauer, and Shakespeare? Much more than to publishers and interested friends I owe, and they owe, gratitude to these men who made their own names live, and made life better for their special energy spent among us. Looking back from this foreword (which ought to be at the end of the book) I think these poets have merely found, in these pages, another way to speak. My part is now obvious: I say, listen!

THE POET'S WORK

THE POET'S WORDS

THE poet's work is to find words for the sense of
life which he learns more and more surely to recognize in himself. Some people need to build ships,
fences, or footstools. Some people need to dance,
or have children, or play games of strength and
speed. Some need to act, or paint; some to fight, or
sell; or collect facts, books, or money. They express
as they may the sense of life that demands expression. A good poet (the streets are full of bad poets)
probably finds deep enduring pleasure, too, in doing
some of these things, because he is really different
from other men in but one way. That difference is
his use of words to satisfy his continuous creative
needs.

At first the poet will delight in all words, any
words that grow on the page, thinking that they
represent his sense of life. When the young poet
recovers from blind reverence for his own words,
because they are his words, and therefore sacred,
then he begins to grow. If he is not one whose merely
healthy energy at one passing age releases itself in
writing, and then moves on to other things, he will
become profoundly uncomfortable about all the
words he has written, and this will grow to still
darker dissatisfaction. Midnight vows, and muttered
curses at the heaviness of his hand on paper will
slowly, though he does not know it, lighten the dark

and ease the hurt. He will wish to write only the best words, the words his ear chooses, the words his unique and secret pulse requires. He teaches himself discrimination in words, alert more and more, as he grows, for the sound of the just, the right, the only word in its place for his feeling and thought. At this stage of his labours (lonely, angry, happy, proud, miserable) he admires the pace and colour of the words of other poets. He imitates them, though he desires a style all his own. But out of this long workmanship he is bringing a new combination of the best he knows beyond his own page, the best he himself has done, and best he knows he will do. Suddenly he learns from some articulate reader that he has created a new style, recognizable and approved. Then the poet knows that his work, to which no one but himself has yet given time and foresight and courage, has been successful. He begins to believe that it will be possible to record his world, within and around him, and his sense of the life of it.

In trying to explain what primitive men might have felt about the man of words, we now please ourselves with imagining the tribes, fearful of wordy magic, murmuring uneasily at the first poet's imitation of real action. But it must have begun that way. The art of poetry lies in imitation by words, and in the pleasure of play with words, in its first age. Perhaps of all man's imitations the dance is the most deeply and simply instinctive. A dumb man can dance, or make his hands and face dance the story out. The dance, too, had a pattern which could

be remembered and repeated. But when there was
language, words could be made to move in imitation
of that action, with the exact posture, the same swiftness, the same satisfaction in rhythm. At last, when
the words themselves came to have such rolling re-
verberations of meaning, such ghostly genealogies
of memory, such Saturn-rings of light around them,
all the dance was in the words. Poetry had become
words. The words had become life.

Now with our tens of thousands of words we
may, as John Donne said, 'knocke, breathe, shine, and
seeke to mend'. We may, as he prayed, batter the
heart. Donne himself, 'in whose words there is such
height of figures, such peregrinations to fetch remote
and precious metaphors', knew how to storm the
imagination with thundering phrases and strange
devices of the language. His vehement and tragic
mind must have found great though brief content,
writing sermons in the dean's study at St. Paul's. It
was not wholly a churchly delight, either, not only
a pastor's anxiety to teach his congregation, that
fetched words onto paper like those of his Christmas
evening service in 1624. He spoke then of God's
bounty. 'If some King of the earth', he wrote, 'have
so large an extent of Dominion, in North, and South,
as that he hath Winter and Summer together in his
Dominions, so large an extent East and West, as that
he hath day and night together in his Dominions,
much more hath God mercy and judgement together: He brought light out of darknesse, not out
of a lesser light; he can bring thy Summer out of

Winter, though thou have no Spring; though in the wayes of fortune, or understanding, or conscience, thou have been benighted till now, wintred and frozen, clouded and eclypsed, damped and benummed, smothered and stupified till now, now God comes to thee, not as in the dawning of the day, not as in the bud of the spring, but as the Sun at noon to illustrate all shadows, as the sheaves in harvest, to fill all penuries, all occasions invite his mercies, and all times are his seasons.' These rolling, mounting Elizabethan cadences are probably some of the most satisfying public words a poet ever prepared and delivered. We may not doubt that Donne's passionate sincerity impelled them. But we may be sure that he gloried, as a lyric poet passed from the weather of his youth to the more threatening weather of middle age, in these sheer cataracts and cascades, this surf, this rising gale and stormy sky of language for its own sake.

No satisfaction, for the poet, equals the satisfaction of springing at last the obstinate words into the stubborn line. No matter how clearly-drawn his system of thought, no matter how extravagant his emotion, still the poet warms to the word. Still he smiles alone as a carver will at some cut that makes of skill and luck and inspiration a new shape in the world. The dangers are very great. Words will diminish and die, or change to offend the ears of another generation. Some overtone harmonized with whatever honest cunning may in the course of time turn all the rest to discord. The rewards are also great. Words may outlive generations of men and come enriched to the newest readers of all time. The poet has an almost medical sense for healthy words that have the seeds of poems in them. To work in words, knowing their present excellence, and fore-knowing their immortality, is itself an enduring satis-faction. And there is the harder, more actual life in words, when the writer stands up on his feet and builds, and we see it and hear it; as Carlyle said, 'Wonderful it is with what cutting words, now and then, he severs asunder the confusion; shears it down, were it furlongs deep, into the true center of the matter; and there not only hits the nail on the head, but with crushing force smites it home, and buries it.'

It is said, and romantically said, that language was once upon a time all poetry, pure in its sym-bolism, and strong and exact, and that the ages have dulled and blackened it. But it is nonsense to sup-pose that a current language cannot become, through art, worthy of and part of the great tradition. We like to mourn saying that the freedom, brevity, vigour, and resonance of the Elizabethans was supe-rior to anything we write now. But where could the great tradition be, if it were living at all, and not be here and now? We may or we may not accept the language of the age; what we must not accept of any age are the counterfeit, the shoddy, the ill-nourished words. Ten to one a word will endure further because it has already lasted. But this is the sort of word that has gathered association, not the

word that with much handling has blurred and begun to crumble. Every language and every age has
both kinds. The poet's labour is one of discrimination.

John Donne for his towering sermons and the
black hammer of his mind that beat and shaped
them upward, and Shakespeare for the bright, trembling flow and flight of his imagery, and Montaigne,
and Carlyle, for their different passionate reasons,
would have waked to the words of Gerard Manley
Hopkins. Hopkins has brought with his new vivid
shapes and sounds more astonishment and envious
despair to the minds of later poets than any writer.
It was Hopkins who wrote 'the widow-making
unchilding unfathering deeps'. It was Hopkins who
wrought this tremendous hyphenation to describe
the falcon 'in his riding of the rolling level underneath him steady air'; who said he woke later than
moonrise 'in the white and the walk of the morning';
who called ancient Oxford 'towery city and branchy
between towers; cuckoo-echoing, bell-swarméd,
lark-charméd, rook-racked, river-rounded'. He did
what any poet would wish to do. With the work of
his mind he stretched language to reach up to and
enclose new sights, wider thoughts, more vivid
experience. He was a poet who worked slowly,
writing little (or rejecting much) and testing his
words through silent years, till he could join them
to create his sense of the world.

When the words have been put together, and
words so plain in themselves matched to make phrases

like 'this goodly frame, the earth . . . this majestic roof fretted with golden fire', or 'else a great Prince in prison lies', or 'I also bear a bell-branch full of ease', then falls that inexplicable radiance on the page, and round the room where the page is read, that is called poetry. It has taken more than words to do this, to be sure. There was an urgency in the poet that brimmed and he could not help it; it overflowed and he was glad. The nature of that urgency may be decided in another place by other more painstaking methodical probers and examiners. We can be sure only that unless that surge of wonder, that intolerable beating of wings in the poet's mind, had found the right words, we never should have cared. There is poetry in words, much blood in words, but there is a thing that moves behind them, a spirit that puts them on like a garment and wears them, filling the infinite possibilities of their drapery with a body that lives and moves, and goes up and down to delight us with its grace and stir us with its vigour.

'GRANT ME BUT DECENT WORDS'

Then there arose a masterless man, one who had taken no part in the action of his fellows, who had no special virtue, but who was afflicted—that is the phrase—with the magic of the necessary word. He saw, he told, he described the merits of the notable deed in such a fashion, we are assured, that the words 'became alive and walked up and down in the hearts of all his hearers.'

Rudyard Kipling, *A Book of Words*

Poetry is words. It is a certain way of using words, so that they take on a vitality which they have in no other use of them. Every significance which words can carry in speech or prose is intensified in poetry— quality of sound, shades of meaning, symbolic importance—but as well as this sharpening of value, there is a creation of new values, which belong to the poetic use of words alone. They work with a secret potency, they take on a new personality. They may not be distinguished or unusual, at all; indeed, they can be of the barest simplicity. But their choice and ordering seem inevitable; they create a harmony, a security, a conviction.

Elizabeth Drew, *Discovering Poetry*

It is the spirit that quickeneth; the flesh profiteth nothing: the words that I speak unto you, they are spirit, and they are life.

St. John, VI. 63

He drew forth a phrase from his treasure and spoke it softly to himself:

'—a day of dappled seaborne clouds—'

The phrase and the day and the scene harmonized in a chord. Words. Was it their colours? He allowed them to glow and fade, hue after hue: sunrise gold, the russet and green of apple orchards, azure of waves, the gray-fringed fleece of clouds. No, it was

not their colours: it was the poise and balance of the
period itself. Did he then love the rhythmic rise and
fall of words better than their association of legend
and colour? Or was it that, being as weak of sight
as he was shy of mind, he drew less pleasure from the
reflection of the glowing sensible world through the
prism of a language many-coloured and richly
storied than from the contemplation of an inner
world of individual emotions mirrored perfectly in
a lucid supple periodic prose?

James Joyce, *Portrait of the Artist as a Young Man*

Poetry is a function of language, recording, vivify-
ing, correcting word and idiom, like a purification of
the blood-streams of nations. As long as people are
talking, exchanging new words and evolving a new
idiom, poetry is an essential activity of life. If this
function is not performed, language, literature, and
hence, ultimately, humanity, suffer.

Stephen Spender, *The Artistic Future of Poetry*

Grant me, O ye powers which touch the tongue
with eloquence in distress—whatever is my cast,
Grant me but decent words to exclaim in, and I will
give my nature way.   Lawrence Sterne

I would be willing to throw away everything else
but that: enthusiasm tamed by metaphor. Let me
rest the case there. I do not think anybody ever
knows the discreet use of metaphor, his own or other
people's, unless he has been properly educated in
poetry.   Robert Frost, *Education by Poetry*

Communication is health; communication is truth; communication is happiness. To share is our duty; to go down boldly and bring to light those hidden thoughts which are most diseased; to conceal nothing; to pretend nothing; if we are ignorant to say so; if we love our friends to let them know it.

Virginia Woolf, 'Montaigne', *The Common Reader*

The written word
Should be clean as a bone,
Clear as light,
Firm as stone.
Two words are not
As good as one.

Anonymous

Verbs and words derived from verbs are of great importance. When you say that your object does something, rather than that it is something or like something else, you give it life and movement. Nouns stand for ideas, names and things. Each noun is a complete picture. Nouns and verbs are almost pure metal. Adjectives are cheaper ore; they have less strength of meaning, since they stand for just one aspect of a thing, one characteristic, and do not represent it in its entirety.

Marie Gilchrist, *Writing Poetry*

. . . words that have been
So nimble and so full of subtle flame
As if that everyone from whence they came

Had meant to put his whole wit in a jest
And had resolved to live a fool the rest
Of his dull life.
                    Francis Beaumont, 'To Ben Jonson'

You must know that words like *charm* and *enchantment* will not do; the thought is of beauty as of something that can be physically kept and lost, and by physical things only, like keys; then the things must become *mundus muliebris*; and thirdly, they must not be very markedly old-fashioned. You will see that this limits the choice of words very much indeed.

Gerard Manley Hopkins, XCIII,
Letters to Robert Bridges

Ye knowe eek that in forme of speche is chaunge
Within a thousand yeer, and wordes tho
That hadden pris, now wonder nyce and straunge
Us thinketh hem, and yet thei spak hem so,
And sped as well in love as men now do.
        Geoffrey Chaucer, *Troilus and Criseyde*

Nay all speech, even the commonest speech, has something of song in it; not a parish in the world but has its parish-accent;—the rhythm or tune to which the people there sing what they have to say! Accent is a kind of chanting; all men have accent of their own—though they notice only that of others.
Thomas Carlyle, 'The Hero as Poet', *On Heroes,
Hero-Worship, and the Heroic in History*

Unspoken, a half-forgotten line flashed through his mind. Where had he read that, or heard it? Oxford, Carlisle, The Highlands, Avignon? 'We are lost, Queen Honour—' How did it go? '. .Queen Honour is the deathless—' Who said that? How could he have forgotten? '. .a battered rascal guard still closes round her.'

Eugene Manlove Rhodes, *The Trusty Knave*

Into this wild ocean of words Shakespeare plunged head over heels, and disported himself in it with a wild dolphin joy. He collected words from everywhere, from rustic speech and dialect (he no doubt spoke the Warwickshire dialect all his life), from Chaucer and the old books, from translators of the classics, from lawyers and grave theologians, from travelled young gallants. He was, moreover, perhaps the greatest word-creator the world has ever known, and has probably added more new words to our vocabulary than all the other English poets put together. He made up his language as he went along—'crashing', as he has been described, 'through the forest of words like a thunderbolt, crushing them out of shape if they don't fit in, melting moods and tenses, and leaving people to gape at the transformation.'

Logan Pearsall Smith, *On Reading Shakespeare*

Hands, do what you're bid:
Bring the balloon of the mind

That bellies and drags in the wind
Into its narrow shed.
William Butler Yeats, 'The Balloon of the Mind'
The Wild Swans at Coole

When Coleridge composed—in a dream, as he alleged—

> In Xanadu did Kubla Khan
> A stately pleasure-dome decree,
> Where Alph, the sacred river, ran
> Through caverns measureless to man,
> Down to a sunless sea

was he aware that, as Stevenson showed later on, he was running hard, all through, a certain chord or group of letters—KANDLSR, the first being built on a kind of framework of KANDL, the second on KDLSR, the third on all the letters of the chord, the fourth on KANSLR, and the fifth on NDLS? Did he chop and change words in his dream, perhaps using at first the word 'sombre' in the third line, and then saying, 'No, I must work in that K and D,' and so substituting the word 'sacred?'

We may well doubt that. Quite as probably he just kept turning each line over and over in his mind in some form which it took first, felt something gritty or obstructive here and there—perhaps in 'sombre'— mused over possible alternative words, and feeling, when he tried 'sacred', that the grit was gone, popped the word in, and there an end, without any consciousness of having stuck stoutly to the chord KANDLSR, and having escaped the seductions of

the rival chord SMBR (which sounds like a useful dominant for an Ode to September). But there the strong consonantal skeleton is, however it came in.
C. E. Montague, 'Easy Reading, Hard Writing'
A Writer's Notes on His Trade

To win the secret of words, to make a phrase that would murmur of summer and the bee, to summon the wind into a sentence, to conjure the odour of the night into the surge and fall and harmony of a line; this was the tale of the long evenings, of the candleflame white upon the paper and the eager pen.   Arthur Machen, *The Hill of Dreams*

No doubt the time will come when psychology will tell us exactly what does happen within our consciousness when a certain collection of words seizes upon us and sends a dazzle of glory rushing through our veins; or a haunting sweetness ringing in our ears; or brings a shock of surprised delight to our eyes; or kindles a glowing warmth about the heart; or brings us tears. At present we only know that when we read:

> Lift up your heads, O ye gates, and be
> lift up, ye everlasting doors: and
> the King of Glory shall come in.

or

> The horns of Elfland faintly blowing.

or

> And hearken to the birds' love-learned song
> The dewy leaves among.

or
> And mighty poets in their misery dead.

or
> Everyone suddenly burst out singing.

or
> He is dead and gone, lady.

a certain sense of enchantment fastens upon many of us. Not, of course, upon everyone. There is always the examinee who paraphrased

> Heard melodies are sweet, but those unheard
> Are sweeter

as 'it is nice to listen to music, but nicer not to.' But for anyone who possesses a 'sense of words', which is the same thing as the sense of poetry, a certain leaping of attention takes place, a brightening of the inward eye, a flame of response.

Elizabeth Drew, Discovering Poetry

>   . . . but his ears
> Were filled with voices, filled with a sound of
>   singing,
> The wind's voice from the mountain; and his
>   heart
> Radiant in his breast was like a lamp . . .
> And from that time his house was dark no more,
> But housed an angel who was silent there,
> Beating bright wings, yet moveless; and the light
> Went forth from him; although he said no word.

> Conrad Aiken, **XXXIX**, *Preludes for Memnon*

She waited. Her husband spoke. He was repeating something, and she knew it was poetry from the rhythm and the ring of exultation and melancholy in his voice.

Virginia Woolf, *To the Lighthouse*

But other men long after he is dead,
Seeing these hills, will catch their breath and
  stare:
As one who, reading in a book some word
That calls joy back, but can recall not where—
Only a crazy sweetness in the head—
Will stare at the black print till the page is
  blurred.

Archibald MacLeish, 'Pony Rock'
Poems 1924-1933

. . . something I cannot describe, but know to myself by the inadequate word *terrible pathos*— something of what you call temper in poetry: a right temper which goes to the point of the terrible: the terrible crystal.

Richard Watson Dixon, XXA,
Correspondence with Gerard Manley Hopkins

Most rhythms are made up as much of disappointments and postponements and surprises and betrayals as of simple straightforward satisfactions.

I. A. Richards, 'Rhythm and Metre'
Principles of Literary Criticism

What I have been after from the first, consciously
and unconsciously, is tones of voice. I've wanted to
write down certain brute throat noises so that no one
could miss them in my sentences. I have been guilty
of speaking sentences as a mere notation for indi-
cating them. They have been my observation and
my subject-matter.

Robert Frost, *from notes on a lecture*

The verse-rhythm of Donne's poetry is the natural
and outward form of his mental temper . . . In
Donne, the meaning, straining against the rhythm
of the fore-established metre in the reader's mind,
reproduces there the slow, tense emphasis of Donne's
thought. The melodists, from Greene and Marlowe
to Swinburne, are always in danger (if it is a danger)
of lulling the mind to sleep with the music of the
verse. The verse pattern is caught at once. . . .
Donne's verse is never lyric in this sense. Instead he
leaves you, line after line and phrase after phrase,
in doubt of the pattern, or of how the line is to be
fitted to the pattern, producing thereby a searching
pause on almost every syllable—a sort of perpetual
'hovering accent.'

H. M. Belden, *Donne's Prosody*

You must evolve a set of counters or abstractions
or allegories which will bear the inflection of the
times without relying on the fashionable accent of
the moment. . . . Not the well-rounded phrase-
making which is only the trade-mark of verse, but

that untheatrical tone, that compelling pitch which
cannot be defined and cannot be mistaken.

Louis Untermeyer, ' "Poets to Come!" '
Play in Poetry

Before man came to blow it right
　　The wind once blew itself untaught,
And did its loudest day and night
　　In any rough place where it caught.

Man came to tell it what was wrong:
　　It hadn't found the place to blow;
It blew too hard—the aim was song.
　　And listen—how it ought to go!

He took a little in his mouth,
　　And held it long enough for north
To be converted into south,
　　And then by measure blew it forth.

By measure. It was word and note,
　　The wind the wind had meant to be—
A little through the lips and throat.
　　The aim was song—the wind could see.

Robert Frost, 'The Aim Was Song'
New Hampshire

Wonderful it is with what cutting words, now
and then, he severs asunder the confusion; shears it
down, were it furlongs deep, into the true centre
of the matter; and there not only hits the nail on the
head, but with crushing force smites it home, and
buries it.　　Thomas Carlyle, *Sartor Resartus*

If we cannot say why we capitulate thus, we may at least try to fix and describe the sensations that visit us while the charm is at work.

For one thing, we are deeply excited. We are shaken or lifted out of our ordinary state of consciousness. Many of our faculties are, for the moment, enhanced. We feel keener perceptions coming into action within us. We are given the use of more than our normal stock of penetrative sympathy: we feel that we can enter into people's feelings, and understand the quality of their lives better than ever before.

Another effect of the drug is that, while it is acting strongly, the whole adventure of mankind upon the earth gains, in our sight, a new momentousness, precariousness, and beauty. The new and higher scale of power in ourselves seems to be challenged by an equal increase in the size of the objects on which it is exercised. Living becomes a grander affair than we had ever thought.

A third effect on the mind is a powerful sense— authentic or illusory—of being in the presence of extraordinary possibilities. You feel as if new doors of understanding and delight were beginning to open around you. Some sort of mysterious liberation or empowerment seems to be approaching. You are assured, in an unaccountable way, that wonderful enlightenments, still unreceived, are on their way to you, like new stars that are nearing the point in space at which they will come within range of our sight.

These sensations may not be defined or measured as closely as doctors measure a patient's temperature, his pulse, and his blood pressure. And yet they are worth describing, if only because you will find that you are also describing something else by the way. The nearer you get to saying just what you feel, when under the spell of great writing, the nearer you are, too, to defining the state of mind and heart in which great things are written.

C. E. Montague, 'The Last Question of All'
A Writer's Notes on His Trade

Shakespeare does not confine himself, like many poets, only to visual images; he makes use of impressions from the other senses, the senses of smell and hearing; and seems to have been especially fond of images of reverberating sound, trumpets and horns and the baying of hounds from afar. Motor images, as they are called, sensations of effort, strain, movement, of rushing winds or horses, are frequent in his poetry, and also of the sea ('surge' is a favorite word with Shakespeare) and of the flow of rivers, as in one of his most splendid images, of the Pontic sea.

Logan Pearsall Smith, *On Reading Shakespeare*

. . . for freedom, for brevity, and for vigour, Elizabethan is superior to modern English. Many of the words employed by Shakespeare and his contemporaries were the recent inventions of the age; hence they are used with a freshness and an exactness to which we are strangers. Again, the spoken

English so far predominated over the grammatical English that it materially influenced the rhythm of the verse, the construction of the sentence, and sometimes the spelling of the words. Hence sprung an artless and unlaboured harmony which seems the natural heritage of the Elizabethan poets, whereas such harmony as is attained by modern authors frequently betrays a painful excess of art. Lastly, the use of some few still remaining inflections (the subjunctive in particular), the lingering sense of many other inflections that had passed away leaving behind something of the old versatility and audacity in the arrangement of the sentence, the stern subordination of grammar to terseness and clearness, and the consequent directness and naturalness of expression, all conspire to give a liveliness and wakefulness to Shakesperian English which are wanting in the grammatical monotony of the present day. We may perhaps claim some superiority in completeness and perspicuity for modern English, but if we were to appeal on this ground to the shade of Shakespeare in the words of Antonio in the Tempest,—

> Do you not hear us speak?

we might fairly be crushed with the reply of Sebastian—

> I do; and surely
> It is a sleepy language.

E. A. Abbott, 'Introduction'
A Shakesperian Grammar

Marlowe was a master of resonance. There are here and there tender passages for a subdued voice in his writings, but for the most part his lines demand 'mouthing' by a good actor, they call for the setting of the stage, they are rhetoric shot through with poetry. Back of the sonority lies violence of passion demanding an outlet in strong words. Marlowe is the swashbuckling Elizabethan, dynamic with the longing for infinite power, as in Tamburlaine; or for endless riches, as in the Jew of Malta; or for all knowledge, as in Dr. Faustus.

M. J. Herzburg, 'Marlowe's Mighty Line'
Word Study

. . . in whose words there is such a height of figures, such peregrinations to fetch remote and precious metaphors, such curtains of allegories, such third heavens of hyperboles.

John Donne, *Sermons*

The reader of Milton must always be on his duty: he is surrounded with sense; it rises in every line; every word is to the purpose. There are no lazy intervals; all has been considered, and demands and merits observation. If this be called obscurity, let it be remembered that it is such obscurity as is a compliment to the reader; not that vicious obscurity which proceeds from a muddled head.

S. T. Coleridge, *Lectures on Shakespeare*

An Elizabethan drama was, as Coleridge perceived in one of the flashes of his dark lantern, 'something between a recitation and a representation;' it was built, as a later critic put it, 'upon the vigour and beauty of speech. We may suppose that at its best the mere speaking of the plays was a very brilliant thing, comparable to *bel canto*, or a pianist's virtuosity.'

> We do it wrong, being so majestical,
> To offer it the show of violence;
> For it is, as the air, invulnerable,
> And our vain blows malicious mockery.
>
> Death, that hath sucked the honey of thy breath,
> Hath had no power yet upon thy beauty:
> Thou art not conquered; beauty's ensign yet
> Is crimson in thy lips and in thy cheeks,
> And death's pale flag is not advancéd there.

Speeches like these were recited to audiences who loved fine language as we love music, and who by no means cared, as we care, for the consistency of character. Plangent declamation, or passages made splendid by this overplus of diction, this fine-broken starlight of fine words, was what they liked.

Logan Pearsall Smith, *On Reading Shakespeare*

Yet even the greatest writers are affected by the intoxication of mere words in the artistry of language. Shakespeare is, constantly, and not content with 'making the green one red', he needs must at the same time 'the multitudinous seas incarnadine.' It is conspicuous in Keats . . . and often, as in 'The Eve of St. Agnes', where he seemed to be concerned with beautiful things, he was really concerned with beautiful words. . . . I recall how Verlaine would sometimes repeat in varying tones some rather unfamiliar word, rolling it round and round in his mouth, sucking it like a sweetmeat, licking the sound into the shape that pleased him; some people may perhaps have found a little bizarre the single words ('Green' for example) which he sometimes made the title of a song, but if they adopt the preliminary Verlanian process they may understand how he had fitted such words to music and meaning.

Havelock Ellis, 'The Art of Writing'
The Dance of Life

Therein lay the manliness of the Elizabethans, they wrote because they enjoyed it: why the sheer villainy of their handwriting shows what fun they had, the words tumbling down in such golden-burning heat they halted not to mend and correct their scrawls and quill-forks.

Christopher Morley, *Inward Ho!*

Theirs, too, is the word-coining genius, as if thought plunged into a sea of words and came up dripping.

Virginia Woolf, 'Notes on An Elizabethan Play'
The Common Reader

The Holy Ghost is an eloquent Author, a vehement, and an abundant Author, but yet not luxuriant; he is a far from penurious, but as far from a superfluous style too.   John Donne, *Sermons*

'When *I* use a word,' Humpty Dumpty said, in rather a scornful tone, 'it means just what I choose it to mean—neither more nor less.'

'The question is,' said Alice, 'whether you *can* make the words mean so many different things.'

'The question is,' said Humpty Dumpty, 'which is to be master—that's all.'

Lewis Carroll, *Through the Looking Glass*

As we go back in history, language becomes more picturesque, until its infancy, when it is all poetry; or all spiritual facts are found represented by natural symbols. The same symbols are found to make the original elements of all languages. It has moreover been observed, that the idioms of all languages approach each other in passages of the greatest eloquence and power. And as this is the first language, so it is the last.

R. W. Emerson, 'Nature', *The Conduct of Life*

In all languages the creation and use of echoic and symbolic words seems to have been on the increase in historical times. If to this we add the selective processes through which words which have only secondarily acquired symbolical value survive at the cost of less adequate expressions, or less adequate forms of the same words, and subsequently give rise to a host of derivatives, then we may say that languages in the course of time grow richer and richer in symbolic words.

Otto Jespersen, *Language*

Every word which is used to express a moral or
intellectual fact, if traced to its root, is found to be
borrowed from some material appearance. Right
means straight; wrong means twisted. Spirit primarily means wind; transgression, the crossing of a
line; supercilious, the raising of an eyebrow. We
say the heart to express emotion, the head to denote
thought; and thought and emotion are words borrowed from sensible things, and now appropriated
to spiritual nature. Most of the process by which
this transformation is made, is hidden from us in
the remote time when language was framed; but
the same tendency may be observed daily in children. Children and savages use only nouns or names
of things, which they convert into verbs, and apply
to analogous mental acts.

R. W. Emerson, 'Nature', *The Conduct of Life*

Under the dream of that stupendous night,
With furious brain, and heart absurdly stout,
I dared to cry my difference to the height;
My way, my love, and words I thought about.

At first my words were sparks that blotted out.
Then miles above a storm of music grew,
And the sky changed, light bloomed, and I heard
    shout
The echoing arches where the sun comes through.

White daylight broke around the airy shores:
My mind pressed hard at every boundary,

Opening taller and more distant doors—
And I had always known how this would be!

John Holmes, 'For the Poet's Birthday'
Address to the Living

The magic of literature lies in words, and not in any man. Witness, a thousand excellent, strenuous words can leave us quite cold or put us to sleep, whereas a bare half-hundred words breathed upon by some man in his agony, or in his exultation, or in his idleness, ten generations ago, can still lead whole nations into and out of captivity, can open to us the doors of the three worlds, or stir us so intolerably that we can scarcely abide to look at our own souls.

Rudyard Kipling, *A Book of Words*

But the finer the poet, the fuller and richer will be the value of his words and the necessary response of the reader. It is not only their surface, but their whole content and substance which has to be savoured; their sound in the ear and their taste and feel in the mouth; a sense of their plasticity and density; their colouring from the past; their echoes and associations; their disposal and manipulation in the poem itself, and all the modifications of their significance which arise from that. It is amazing how a single word can make a whole poem by an isolation of it in a special use which brings a throb of unexpected discovery.

Elizabeth Drew, *Discovering Poetry*

It was a field that was almost virgin. For Science, according to Victorian ideas, as a subject for Poetry, had been almost completely taboo. Poetry must be 'poetical' (in the bad old sense of that really impossible word): but all these new things—the inventions of science and scientific processes and scientific terminology—were exactly the reverse. They were 'practical'. They were too new to have acquired even a suspicion of glamour. Consequently if a poet touched them at all, he must do so with the utmost circumspection. Think, for instance, of Tennyson's difficulties in the 'Princess':

> A dozen angry models jetted steam:
> A petty railway ran: a fire-balloon
> Rose gem-like up before the dusky grives
> And dropt a fairy parachute and past:
> And there thro' twenty posts of telegraph
> They flashed a saucy message to and fro
> Between the mimic stations; so that sport
> Went hand in hand with Science . . .

It has a monstrous archness. Subject and expression are not fused and interfused. They go uneasily together. But turn to a modern poet, who accepts all the component parts of modern life as natural and therefore stuff out of which poetry is to be made:

> After the first powerful plain manifesto
> The black statement of pistons, without more fuss
> But gliding like a queen, she leaves the station.
>
> Beyond the town there lies the open country
> Where, gathering speed, she acquires mystery,
> The luminous self-possession of ships on ocean.

It is now she begins to sing—at first quite low
Then loud, and at last with a jazzy madness—
The song of her whistle screaming at curves,
Of deafening tunnels, brakes, innumerable bolts,
And always light, aerial, underneath
Goes the elate metre of her wheels.

(Stephen Spender)

Here all the material, the awkward facts, the embarrassing new things of the new world, have been unconditionally accepted and absorbed. And therefore it comes out a homogeneous whole, naturally and inevitably transmuted into poetry.

Martin Gilkes, *A Key to Modern English Poetry*

Peculiar, not far-fetched; natural, but not obvious; delicate, not affected; dignified, not swelling; fiery, but not mad; rich in imagery, but not loaded with it—in short, a union of harmony and good sense, of perspicuity and conciseness. Thought is the body of such an ode, enthusiasm the soul, and imagery the drapery.

S. T. Coleridge, *Anima Poetae*

THE POET'S KNOWLEDGE

THE poet who is an artist makes it the work of his lifetime to find the inner rhythm which makes him different from all men, and to perfect the transmission of that rhythm to them. His difficulties and triumphs, failures and explanations of them, his allies, his enemies, and above all his actual skill in performance, are what the poet meditates most after he has come of age in his art. It is one thing to see the glories of the world with an eye that magnifies them to the spirit; it is another to control that change. Both things are necessary, by whatever name we call them, for the poet's purpose; understanding of both is necessary to the readers of poetry.

The labour a poet performs in making poetry is endless, difficult, lonely, and, when rightly concluded, more deeply satisfying than any other work. Unless, as he sometimes suspects, that work is architecture. What is he trying to do, that he is willing to endure some public neglect and much private bafflement for the sake of scattered victories? Is he trying to establish communication across the loneliness that separates man and man? Is he trying to discover some time-resisting substance that will contain his soul and so let him live forever? Is he crying round the town for the world to know some news of beauty he is too generous to keep to himself? Is he consecrating himself to the art of doing these things, unselfishly, yet thoughtless of others? A little of all, and all of none. Most of the time he is simply trying to get the thing right that he is doing. In a world where many men have no work to do, or hate the work they must do to live, the poet is happy. He has his work. To say he is devoted to the high cause of truth is true, but he does not speak in that exalted language; ministers do not talk of God at lunch. The nature of poetry makes it possible to speak of him thus, perhaps, but of his own work as an artist the poet would say that he is trying to do the job right as he sees it, for its own sake.

Manipulation of the word in the line scarcely has an end, and while he has it to do he is happy. It fills all his conscious mind, and he brings to his problem part of an answer from every experience. Not that he seeks experience for the answer, but he gives himself to it. He knows how durable a satisfaction lies hard in the hand, actual with weight, when every excursion returns him to some unfinished work with words. He is free of the shadow of boredom. He has light on the long task of stripping away from his own spirit, as much as from the half-made poem, all the husks that hide its outline, until the form stands forth. The very concentration of this work sometimes creates its own share of the perfected poem. The ultimate degree of heat needed to melt the heart and mind into active skill comes at the moment of making, and not until then; he writes better than he knows how. Otherwise it is struggle. Hazlitt says it is not like painting, where the painter contends only with nature. But for a while, before the words find their perfect order, when it seems as though they will with one more right epithet or rhyme be done, there is a feeling that the air is full of infinite possibility. But writing poetry is a contention with inner man as well as with outer world, and there is always more to learn about not being defeated.

His teachers are the poets alive before him and with him. But after a certain apprenticeship, he must teach himself or stop learning. When he is a young man, he is curious about poets as people: where did they grow up and go to school? what accident got their first poems into print? who helped them and what delayed them? were they married or not, and were they happy so? were they sick or well, and who were their friends, and where did they sit to talk?—no question is too trivial. The answers to all of them are patiently fitted like parts of a picture puzzle into a map, which will with suitable coloring and alterations of boundaries become a chart of his own career. At first it is of importance to know that Coleridge walked the hills with William and Dorothy Wordsworth, or that Browning had to steal his wife from her father, or that Yeats was active and influential in politics. There must be significance for him in the facts that Hopkins became a priest, and that Robert Frost refused to finish a college course, and that T. S. Eliot, born in St. Louis, lives a royalist, a classicist, and an Anglican in London. From such facts the poet learns, because he compares with such circumstances the writing these men did then and later. He sees that to be a poet is infinitely more than to write and publish a volume. It is a way of life, and a way with life.

As he perfects his own geography, he is more concerned with actual poetry. As he succeeds a little here with his lines, and fails much elsewhere, he learns to estimate the integrities and urgencies that lie behind the volume of collected works, or the volume of life and letters over which he pores. Anecdotes merely illustrate a truth, but no longer contain one. He comes to realize a standard below which he himself may not fall, and conceives some ultimate to which he vows to lift that standard; he is driven with desire to taste the satisfaction in achievement he has read about. From then on he must be his own teacher. Whether his books are read and remembered or not is his responsibility now to himself. If he puts his self-knowledge and the limit of his craftsmanship and the best of his human understanding into them, he will accept the result.

It is the sum of what he teaches himself that determines his quality, which in turn foretells the result. In the midst of external activity, he may, like Yeats rehearsing a play, perceive suddenly that 'tragedy must always be a drowning and breaking of the dykes that separate man from man', and from that time on be able to write tragedy. Or he may gradually come to place, like George Moore, the capacity for revision of the written page above all virtues. He may learn Mozart's lesson that 'when

I am feeling well and in good humor, thoughts come
in swarms and with marvelous ease', or that that
may not be at all his condition for getting things
done. Analogies may teach him, if he has the eye
for them, like the one Hazlitt drew between the
writer and the Indian juggler of knives. Or because
of his knowledge of poetry of the past, he may discover that a contemporary has by adapting or ac-
cepting or exaggerating old methods fashioned a
new one. Failure teaches him that all failure in the
arts may possibly be mended in the next attempt.
Praise teaches him how imperfectly he has transmitted himself, so unpredictable and often so absurd
praise is. All pronouncements on style by artists of
his own generation, of those years ago, help him
shape the idea of his own, for he knows that his style
must be his own or nothing. He learns, by experiences he would hardly care to tell, what medicine
cures or eases for him the old unwillingness to make
the imaginative effort. The weather of his mind,
he knows, is an affair of low pressure areas and sudden storms, which he must learn to predict with unfailing accuracy. He watches the least stirring of
leaves that indicates a rising wind, and he knows
what planets draw his tides. He supports the findings
of an almost instrumental skill in this kind of self-
knowledge with an old native wisdom of intuition
and shrewd speculation. Time concerns him, that
he may not waste it. No waking day is ever quite
long enough. But eventually he learns whether he
must hurry with his life and writing or not. He feels

his own sense of time mysteriously regulating his days. He comes to trust that sense, for it will tell him when to wait, when to act, and it tells him that life will be as long as he requires for his work. At last he learns what all great artists know, each in his kind, to hold to a single ruthless purpose, and that purpose poetry.

The object of this unwearying study is to write poetry that will represent his peculiar inner rhythms, so confirmed and set free that it will speak, original and significant, in the poetry of his age. And who will know whether or not he has succeeded? He will know. That is his greatest satisfaction, even though he may have found readers who have been pleased and changed by poetry he has written. He knows, too, that other poets will know. He has learned to value most the praise of equals, and next the confidence of living men. 'The oration is to the orator,' said Whitman, 'the acting is to the actor and actress, not to the audience.' The poet values their response because they understand as artists, not only the finished thing, but the rigours of devotion to the art.

In spite of much example to the contrary, the poet learns that not all the artistry in the world avails unless his life as a human being is fulfilled and integrated. No man, whatever his purpose, can give himself to it wholly if he has made wrong committments, and wastes time and strength in anxiety over them, finding them unendurable and inescapable. The great artist could not squander his life; lesser artists reveal

themselves by doing so. Just as the poet searches
everywhere and all the time for more knowledge of
his task as poet, he will apply himself to strengthen-
ing his position as man, citizen, husband, and father.
Beneath the surface of life lies a pattern of order. No
one can ignore its shape once it has been revealed,
and no one, without partial but continuous harm,
may live contrary to its direction and harmony. A
man cannot be a good artist and a bad citizen, a
strong poet and a weak human being, or if he is, the
strain and twisting shows surely.

The artist who is a poet has enemies and allies,
some within himself, and some, the least important,
outside himself. The indifferent, the stubborn, the
wilfully blind never cease reproducing themselves,
and they are the enemies of art, dangerous whether
passive or active. But the temptation to publish what
will satisfy nearly everyone, and not, in his own
heart, himself, is the poet's more immediate danger.
Time is always a potential enemy. In merciless and
unforeseen ways Time destroys all but the best and
the most honest poetry. Victory over the temptation to haste can conquer both indifference and
Time. Sudden inspiration, completing the poem, is
a treacherous friend, for it glosses the surface with
what seems to be the light of poetry. But the light
fades and the workmanship loosens in its joints, and
the poem that creation without toil had fashioned
falls apart. The waste of emptiness may threaten,
but here, as Ben Jonson says, 'the mind is like a bow,
the stronger by being unbent.' Infertile hours are

not failure or defeat, but a part of the process of writing, a process that has, like green things growing, spaces of rest. Danger may come from an excess of loyalty to some one method, or poet, or audience, to some habit, or party, or subject, till proportion is destroyed. The complex pull of affections, duties, or pleasures in life as a plain citizen may also distort artistry; since these things go very deep, one or another is sometimes the most corruptive enemy of all, having place and power within and without. It is an expensive but important chapter in the poet's history that tells how he learned to adjust his poetic to his private life, and both to his life in public. It is a story of unfailing renewal of an exact balance between the three. Allies in the poet's self-preservation are his self-respect as an artist, the attraction of the goal still before him, and the height of his old vows. In composition his allies serve with vital allegiance, but not always with their presence when it is most fervently asked. Health and peace of mind are his allies, too; or lacking them, the drive of such a necessity from within that the writing gets done— but this is costly. Knowledge of life and of all poetry are obviously a loyal part. Mastery of his creative powers is something he has learned slowly and thoroughly, and can usually summon to the endeavour, and control. But the support of the unconscious mind, while powerful, is unpredictable. In the crisis a memory of things he had forgotten may rush in, and a knowledge of things he never learned.

Neither in defeat nor in achievement is the poet

unattended. Enemies and allies serve or threaten, and he learns that he does not live to himself. He must look before and after, and keep his lantern lighted at his belt, along the road he has been sent, no matter how many others shine from the darkness ahead of him, or come winking alone behind.

What every artist knows is that his work is never done. So long as he is conscious (and the poet is known for his supreme consciousness) he is bound to life and art, and has been pulling the knot tighter all the time. They go three together, and he is the one least willing to part company. If with all his pondering and practice of craftsmanship, his untiring adjustment of the necessities of writing to the necessities of living, and his accompaniment by enemy and ally to the blank white paper, he writes at last ten living lines, does he then retire clutching laurel? He knows better than anyone that he does not. In the next poem he may write twelve lines as good or better, and even if it is only five more, he is willing (he cannot help himself) to try until then—and a little further.

'THE GREAT AND GOLDEN RULE'

She remembered, all of a sudden as if she had found a treasure, that she had her work. In a flash she saw her picture, and thought, Yes, I shall put the tree further in the middle; then I shall avoid that awkward space. That's what I shall do. She took

up the salt-cellar and put it down again on a flower
in the pattern in the table-cloth, so as to remind
herself to move the tree.

Virginia Woolf, To the Lighthouse

In the one case, the colours seem breathed on the
canvas as by magic, the work and wonder of a moment: in the other, they seem inlaid in the body of
the work, and as if it took the artist years of unremitting labour, and of delightful never-ending progress to perfection. Who would ever wish to come
to the close of such works,—not to dwell on them,
to return to them, to be wedded to them at the last?

William Hazlitt, 'On the Pleasure of Painting'
Table Talk

Fly to thy talent! To thy charm!
Thy nest, thine hive, thy sheltering arm!
Who can to sing,
There let him flee;
This is, naught else is, certainty.

James Stephens, Strict Joy

Assimilation and Selection:—When a subject begins to ripen in a poet's mind, the process can be
compared with the expanding of a cell whose walls
gradually become thin and porous and develop, we
might say, a thousand, or a hundred thousand,
mouths. Everything which comes in contact with a
cell so altered can and must serve to nourish it. If it
finds something unsuitable, it closes up or hastily

withdraws; on the other hand it swallows, digests, and assimilates anything which can be made of use to it. And just as such a cell absorbs everything which can contribute to its nourishment, growth, and completion, so a poet's subject draws on all his experiences, knowledge, and emotions for likely material, rejecting and expelling the unadaptable, and continuing gradually to expand until it finally seems to form the entire content of the poet's mind—yes, the poet's mind itself seems transformed into his subject.   Arthur Schnitzler, 'Work and Echo'

Can you doubt that the reason why Shakespeare knew every sound and syllable in the language and could do exactly what he liked with grammar and syntax, was that Hamlet, Falstaff, and Cleopatra rushed him into this knowledge; that the lords, officers, dependents and murderers and common soldiers of the plays insisted that he should say exactly what they felt in words expressing their feelings? It was they who taught him to write, not the begetter of the Sonnets. So that if you want to satisfy all those senses that rise in a swarm whenever we drop a poem among them—the reason, the imagination, the eyes, the ears, the palms of the hands and the soles of the feet, not to mention a million more that the psychologists have yet to name, you will do well to embark upon a long poem in which people as unlike yourself as possible talk at the tops of their voices. And for heaven's sake, publish nothing before you are thirty.

Virginia Woolf, *Letter to a Young Poet*

Nothing goes by luck in composition. It allows of no tricks. The best you can write will be the best you are. Every sentence is the result of a long probation. The author's character is read from title-page to end. Of this he never corrects the proofs.

Thoreau, *Journals*

That pre-existent vision does not exist at all. It only comes into existence while the technical and physical work of painting or writing goes on. To what may end by being a masterpiece an artist may come at first with a mind empty and stone-cold. It may be that 'another common-place model to paint!' was all that Raphael thought as he began the Sistine Madonna. Suppose it is so. Well, he gets out his tackle and starts. In a little while the mere feel of the brush in his hand begins to excite him; the cold engine of his mind is warmed a little; it inclines to move; there kindles in him a faint spark of curiosity about the being who is before him; the quickened mind enlivens the hand, and the brush moves more featly; eagerness is growing in all the employed faculties of the man; images, thoughts, memories, sympathies crowd in upon him till he wonders at himself, with a kind of alarm mixed with delight—will he ever be able to keep himself up to this pitch, he is now so much above par, so strangely endowed, for while it may last, with spiritual insight and also with an unwonted dexterity of hand.

C. E. Montague, 'The Blessing of Adam'
A Writer's Notes on His Trade

What actually happens in a writer's mind when he gets through fiddling and fuming and sits down to tackle the job must always remain a secret between himself and his Demon. The preliminary horrors and shufflings are a valid part of the human comedy. There are innumerable ways of postponing. Some sit on the floor and begin dusting the books on the lower shelves, where they usuallly find 'The Pentecost of Calamity' or 'The Cradle of the Deep' and re-read it entire. Others get into pyjamas and trim their toe-nails, or lock themselves into an office building with a bottle of Bisquit Dubouce. Homer Croy has remarked that his form of trifling is tinkering with his typewriter. 'I have the best-cleaned typewriter in the world,' he says, rather ashamed.

Christopher Morley, 'The Folder'

Every day, every day, my Guide says to me,
Are you ready?
And I say to my Guide, I am ready.
And my Guide says, March.

Anonymous

Poems consciously composed may reach a very high plane, but never so high a one as poems subconsciously composed. It may be said that Keats wrote 'The Triumph of Bacchus;' but that 'The Hymn to Pan' wrote itself. I am not taking into consideration corrections made after the heat of composition is over, because, strange as it may seem, they have almost nothing to do with whether the original draft is done subconsciously or not. A common reason for them is that the subconscious mind dictates too fast for the poet to follow; again, the connection between the subconscious and the conscious minds may break, here and there, leaving holes which the poet must fill as best he can.

Amy Lowell, *John Keats*

It is as if the imagination, seeking for expression, had found both verb and substantive at one rush, had begun to say them almost at once, and had separated them only because the intellect had reduced the original unity into divided but related sounds.

Charles Williams, Introduction to *Poems of Gerard Manley Hopkins*

Moreover, the oddness may make them repulsive at first sight and yet Lang may have liked them on second reading. Indeed, when, on somebody returning me the Eurydice, I opened and read some lines, as one commonly reads whether verse or prose, with the eyes, so to say, only, it struck me aghast with a kind of raw nakedness and unmitigated violence I was unprepared for: but take breath and read it with the ears, as I always wish to read, and my verse becomes all right.

Gerard Manley Hopkins, LIX, *Letters to Robert Bridges*

If you work in a storm of atoms and seconds, if your highest joy is 'life; London; this moment in June' and your deepest mystery 'here is one room; there is another,' then how can you construct your

human beings so that each shall be not a movable
monument but an abiding home, how can you build
between them any permanent roads of love and
hate?

E. M. Forster, 'The Early Novels of Virginia Woolf'
Abinger Harvest

Water colour is swift and immediate in its expression of the artist's emotion. The worst fault of be-
ginners is the desire to copy nature slavishly. Before
you touch colour to paper you should consider
composition and selection carefully. Define the
shapes. Plan your light and dark masses. Then (1)
lay in the dark masses, with a full brush. 'Only in
this manner can you secure a rich bloom.' The dark
masses can be made vibrant by flushing rich colours
together. Add last the colour required to dominate
the mass. (2) After establishing the dark colours,
develop the middle plan. Keep white and brilliances
to the last. Area of white paper held in reserve 'is
a safety hold on the picture'. (3) The final vital stage
is to express your highlights: sunshine and shim-
mers. Sky; foreground; summing-up. If there is
trouble in parts, lay it aside,—or remove the offend-
ing parts by sponging. Purple is the only colour difficult to remove. It stains and holds on like grim death.
A water colour must be painted without fear or fa-
vour, directly, lusciously, with a dripping flowing
colour. To falter is to fail.

Christopher Morley, Review of
Making Water Color by George Ennis

It comes back to me, the whole 'job,' as wonderfully amusing and delightfully difficult from the first; since amusement deeply abides, I think, in any artistic attempt the basis and groundwork of which are conscious of a particular firmness. On that fine hard floor the element of execution feels it may more or less consciously dance; in which case puzzling questions, sharp obstacles, dangers of detail, may come up for it by the dozen without breaking its heart or shaking its nerve. It is the difficulty produced by the loose foundation or the vague scheme that breaks the heart—when a luckless fatuity has over-persuaded an author of the 'saving' virtue of treatment.

Henry James, Preface to *The Awkward Age*

'The better part of godhead is design.
This is not theirs only, for I know mine,
And I project such worlds as need not yield
To this commanded April on the field.

And it is ample. For it satisfies
My royal blood even thus to exercise
The ancestral parts of my theogeny.
I am a god, though none attend to me.'

And he watched, with large head resting in
  the sun,
The gods at play, and did not envy one.
He had his magic, too, and knew his power,
But was too tired to work it in that hour.

John Crowe Ransom, 'Semi-Centennial'
Two Gentlemen in Bonds

A good scene should be, not a picture, but an image. Scene-designing is not what most people imagine it is—a branch of interior decorating. . . . Everything that is actual must undergo a strange metamorphosis, a kind of sea-change, before it can become truth in the theater. There is a curious mystery in this. You will remember the quotation from Hamlet:

> My father—methinks I see my father.
> O where, my lord?
> In my mind's eye, Horatio.

Robert Edmond Jones, *Art in the Theater*

The result of scribbling, the tale of perfect balance, all the elements of the tale understood, and an infinite number of minute adjustments perfectly made, the power of self-criticism fully at work, the shifting surface of word-values and colour in full play, form and rhythmic flow of thought and mood marching forward with the sentences—these are things of a dream, of a dim far day toward which one goes knowing one can never arrive but infinitely glad to be on the road.

Sherwood Anderson, *A Story-Teller's Story*

No work of true genius dares want its appropriate form, neither indeed is there any danger of this. As it must not, so genius can not, be lawless: for it is even this that constitutes genius—the power of acting creatively under laws of its own origination.

S. T. Coleridge, *Lectures on Shakespeare*

To put all that is possible of one's idea into a form and compass that will contain and express it only by delicate adjustments and an exquisite chemistry, so that there will at the end be neither a drop of one's liquor left nor a hair's breadth of the rim of one's glass to spare—every artist will remember how often that sort of necessity has carried with it its particular inspiration.

Henry James, Preface to *The Tragic Muse*

But as air, melody, is what strikes me most of all in music and design in painting, so design, pattern, or what I am in the habit of calling inscape, is what I above all aim at in poetry. Now it is the virtue of design, pattern, or inscape to be distinctive, and it is the vice of distinctiveness to be queer.

Gerard Manley Hopkins, LIII,
Letters to Robert Bridges

We sat together at one summer's end,
That beautiful mild woman, your close friend,
And you and I, and talked of poetry.
I said, 'A line will take us hours maybe;
Yet if it does not seem a moment's thought,
Our stitching and unstitching has been naught.'
       . . . And thereupon
That beautiful mild woman for whose sake
There's many a one shall find out all heartache
On finding that her voice is sweet and low
Replied, 'To be born woman is to know—

Although they do not talk of it at school—
That we must labour to be beautiful.'

William Butler Yeats, 'Adam's Curse'
In the Seven Woods

The great and golden rule of art, as well as of life,
is this:—That the more distinct, sharp, and wiry the
bounding line, the more perfect the work of art: and
the less keen and sharp, the greater is the evidence
of weak imitation, plagiarism, and bungling. . . .
How do we distinguish the oak from the beech, the
horse from the ox, but by the bounding outline?
How do we distinguish one face or countenance
from another, but by the bounding line and its infinite inflections and movements? What is it that
builds a house and plants a garden but the definite
and the determinate? What is it that distinguishes
honesty from knavery but the hard and wiry outline of rectitude and certainty in the actions and intentions? Leave out this line and you leave out life
itself; all is chaos again, and the line of the Almighty
must be drawn out upon it before man or beast can
exist.

William Blake, 'Prose Fragments'

All writers, all artists of any kind, in so far as they
have had any philosophical or critical power, perhaps just in so far as they have been deliberate artists
at all, have had some philosophy, some criticism
of their art; and it has often been this philosophy, or
this criticism, that has evoked their most startling

inspiration, calling into outer life some portion of divine life, or of the buried reality, which could alone extinguish in the emotions what their philosophy or their criticism could extinguish in the intellect.

William Butler Yeats, 'The Symbolism of Poetry'
Ideas of Good and Evil

There are two ways of becoming a writer. One, the cheaper, is to discover a formula; that is black magic; the other is to have the urge; that is white magic.   Carl Van Vechten, *Peter Whiffle*

Critics have observed that considerable writers fall into two classes—(1) those who start with their heads full of great thoughts, and are from the first occupied rather with the matter than with the manner of expressing it. (2) Those who begin with the love of expression and intent to be artists in words, and come through expression to profound thought.

A. Quiller-Couch, 'The Popular Conception of a Poet', *Adventures in Criticism*

There are four prime elements, as I look at it, in all writing, and a fifth which has to exist before good writing is possible.

This fifth element is, of course, the soil from which writing grows—a soil of the mind enriched by observation, experience, and abstract knowledge, rendered fertile by cultivation, and subject to a will to work it. Nothing comes from nothing; and to talk about the practice of writing apart from something to write about is a fallacy which has ruined many otherwise excellent rhetorics. I assume a warm and vigorous soil in this brief discussion of methods, only warning the beginning writer that, until he knows and feels, the fewer words he puts on paper the better for everybody—and, as a writer, he can never know and feel enough.

Henry S. Canby, 'Style', *Designed for Reading*

The one indispensable talent for creative art, whether of the theatre or literature or music or plastic representation, is the talent for experiencing.

Mary Austin, *Everyman's Genius*

It is not enough to have great thoughts before doing the work. The brush stroke at the moment of contact carries inevitably the exact state of being of the artist at the exact moment into the work, and there it is to be seen and read by those who can read such signs, and to be read later by the artist himself with perhaps some surprise, as a revelation of himself.

Robert Henri, *The Art Spirit*

Therefore dive deep into thy bosom; learn the depth, extent, bias, and full fort of thy mind; contract full intimacy with the stranger within thee; excite and cherish every spark of intellectual light and heat, however smothered under former negligence, or scattered through the dull, dark mass of common thoughts; and collecting them into a body, let thy genius rise (if a genius thou hast) as the sun

from chaos; and if I should then say, like an Indian, Worship it (though too bold) yet should I say little more than my second rule enjoins, (viz.) Reverence thyself.   Edward Young,
'Conjectures on Original Composition'

I think what I am after is free meditation. I don't think anybody gets it when he's in anybody's company—only when his soul's alone. I do it when I wake up in the morning. . . . The person who has the freedom of his material is the person who puts two and two together, and the two and two are anywhere out of time and space, brought together.

Robert Frost, *from notes on a lecture*

Great things are done when men and mountains meet;
These are not done by jostling in the street.
William Blake, *Ideas of Good and Evil*

What is necessary to the free man, what is above all necessary to the free writer, is to consider without reference to his enemies the kind of world he himself would like to bring about. That world for all artists, for all men of spirit in a democratic world, the world in which a man is free to do his own work, the world in which a man may think as he pleases, the world in which a man may, with the complete responsibility of a mature individual, control his proper life.   Archibald MacLeish, *Preface to an American Manifesto*

Listen! I will be honest with you;
I do not offer the old smooth prizes, but offer
   rough new prizes;
These are the days that must happen to you:

You shall not heap up what is called riches,
You shall scatter with lavish hand all that
   you earn or achieve,
You but arrive at the city to which you were
   destined—you hardly settle yourself to satisfaction, before you are called by an irresis-
   table urge to depart,
You shall be treated by the ironical smiles
   and mockings of those who remain behind
   you;
What beckonings of love you receive, you
   shall only answer with passionate kisses of
   parting,
You shall not allow the hold of those who
   spread their reached hands toward you.
     Walt Whitman, 'Joy of the Road', *Leaves of Grass*

It is beneath the dignity of poets, the dead and the
living, to accept any praise but that true praise which
is the confidence of living men.

                Hugo von Hofmannsthal,
                'Der Dichter und diese Zeit'

Artists who do not love their art are more numerous, and more unhappy, than we think.
        Logan Pearsall Smith, *Afterthoughts*

Now Intelligence is as much memory as perception; and for it there is always in the transformations
it is watching something familiar which carries it
back to what has already been witnessed, and for-
wards, expectantly, to something it may be going
to witness. Hence to Intelligence there is never mere
repetition, just as there is never utter novelty.

Vernon Lee, *Proteus, or the Future of Intelligence*

To write on their plan it was at least necessary to
read and think. No man could be born a metaphysi-
cal poet, nor assume the dignity of a writer, by descriptions copied from descriptions, by imitations
borrowed from imitations, by traditional imagery
and hereditary similes, by readiness of style and volubility of syllables.

Samuel Johnson, 'Abraham Cowley'
Lives of the Poets

You shall go to your run-out mountain farm,
Poor cast-away of commerce, and so live
That none shall ever see you come to market—
Not for a long time. Plant, breed, produce,
But what you raise or grow, why feed it out,
Eat it or plow it under where it stands
To build the soil. For what is more accursed
Than an impoverished soil pale and metallic?
What cries more to our kind for sympathy?
I'll make a compact with you, Meliboeus,
To match you deed for deed and plan for plan.
Friends crowd around me with their five year plans

That Soviet Russia has made fashionable.
You come to me and I'll unfold to you
A five year plan I call so, not because
It takes ten years or so to carry out,
Rather because it took five years at least
To think it out. Come close, let us conspire—
In self-restraint, if in restraint of trade.
You will go to your run-out mountain farm
And do what I command you. I take care
To command only what you meant to do
Anyway. That is my style of dictator.
Build soil. Turn the farm in upon itself
Until it can contain itself no more,
But sweating-full, drips wine and oil a little.
I will go to my run-out social mind
And be as unsocial with it as I can.
The thought I have, and my first impulse is
To take to market—I will turn it under.
The thought from that thought—I will turn it under.
And so on to the limit of my nature.

Robert Frost, 'Build Soil', *A Further Range*

The enemy has no definite name, though in a certain degree we all know him. He who puts the body before the spirit, the dead before the living: who makes things in order to sell them; who has forgotten that there is such a thing as truth, and measures the world by advertisement or by money; who daily defiles the beauty that surrounds him and makes vulgar the tragedy; whose innermost religion is the worship of the lie in his soul. The Philistine, the vulgarian, the great sophist, the passer of base coin for true, he is all about us, and worse, he has his outposts inside us, persecuting our peace, spoiling our sight, confusing our values, making a man's self seem greater than the race and the present things more important than the eternal. From him and from his influence we find our escape by means of the grammata into that calm world of theirs, where stridency and clamor are forgotten in the ancient stillness, where the strong iron is long since rusted, and the rocks of granite broken into dust, but the great things of the human spirit still shine like stars pointing man's way onward to the great triumph or the great tragedy; and even the little things, the beloved and tender and funny and familiar things, beckon across gulfs of death and change with a magic poignancy, the old things that our dead leaders and forefathers loved, *viva adhuc et desiderio pulcriora*, living still and more beautiful because of our longing.

Gilbert Murray, Religio Grammaticus

I may say that the maker of the world exhausts his skill with each snowflake and dewdrop that he sends down. We think that the one mechanically coheres and that the other simply flows together and falls, but in truth they are the product of enthusiasm, the children of ecstasy, finished with the artist's utmost skill.

Thoreau, Journals

> When I was young,
> I had not given a penny for a song
> Did not the poet sing it with such airs
> That one believed he had a sword upstairs.
> William Butler Yeats, 'All Things Content Me'
> *The Green Helmet*

To write this book well I must believe that it is my only novel and the last book I shall write. I wish to pour all into it without reserve.

André Gide, *Journal*

I feel assured I should write, for the mere yearning and fondness I have for the beautiful, even if my night's labours should be burnt every morning and no eye shine upon them.

John Keats, *Letters*

'Nice? It's the *only* thing,' said the Water Rat solemnly, as he leant forward for his stroke. 'Believe me, my young friend, there is *nothing*—absolutely nothing—half so much worth doing as simply messing about in boats. Simply messing,' he went on dreamily, 'messing—about—in—boats—'

Kenneth Grahame, *The Wind in the Willows*

When I am feeling well and in good humour, thoughts come in swarms and with marvellous ease. Once I catch my air, another comes soon to join it, according to the requirements of the whole composition. Then my mind kindles—the work grows—

I keep hearing it and bring it out more and more clearly, and the composition ends by being completely executed in my mind, however long it may be.

Mozart, *Letters*

We but half express ourselves, and are ashamed of the divine idea which each of us represents. It may be safely trusted as proportionate and of good issues, so it be faithfully imparted, but God will not have his work made manifest by cowards. A man is relieved and gay when he has put his heart into his work and done his best, but what he has said or done otherwise, shall give him no peace. It is a deliverance which does not deliver. In the attempt his genius deserts him; no muse befriends; no invention, no hope.

R. W. Emerson, 'Self-Reliance'

The artist appeals to that part of our being which is not dependent on wisdom; to that in us which is a gift and not an acquisition—and, therefore, more permanently enduring. He speaks to our capacity for delight and wonder, to the sense of mystery surrounding our lives; to our sense of pity, and beauty, and pain.

Joseph Conrad, Preface to
The Nigger of the Narcissus

Nothing is quite beautiful alone; nothing but is beautiful in the whole. A single object is only so far beautiful as it suggests this universal grace. The poet, the painter, the sculptor, the musician, the architect, seek each to concentrate this radiance of the world on one point, and each in his several work to satisfy the love of beauty which stimulates him to produce.

R. W. Emerson, 'Nature'
The Conduct of Life

Whoever absorbs a work of art into himself goes through the same process as the artist who produced it—only he reverses the order of the process and increases its speed.

Friedrich Hebbel, *Tagebücher*

Then for the first time did it strike me that one cannot say anything about a woman. I noticed when they spoke of her, how much they left out, how they mentioned other things—surroundings, localities, objects—and described them up to a certain point where they stopped, stopped quietly, and, as it were, cautiously, just at the delicate outline, never retraced, which enclosed her.

Rainer Maria Rilke,
The Notebook of Malta Laurids Brigge

Tchehov made a mistake in thinking that if he had more time he would have written more fully, described the rain, and the midwife and the doctor having tea. The truth is one can get only so much into a story; there is always a sacrifice. One has to leave out what one knows and longs to use. Why?

I haven't any idea, but there it is. It's always a kind of race to get in as much as one can before it disappears.

Katherine Mansfield, *Journals*

The surest thing there is is we are riders,
And though none too successful at it, guiders,
Through everything presented, land and tide
And now the very air, of what we ride.

What is this talked-of mystery of birth
But being mounted bareback on the earth?
We can just see the infant up astride,
His small fist buried in the bushy hide.

There is our wildest mount—a headless horse.
But though it runs unbridled off its course,
And all our blandishments would seem defied,
We have ideas yet that we haven't tried.

Robert Frost, 'Riders', *West-Running Brook*

I have observed some to make excuses that they cannot express themselves, and pretend to have their fancies full of a great many very fine things, which yet, for want of eloquence, they cannot bring out; a mere shift, and nothing else. Will you know what I think of it? I think they are nothing but shadows of some imperfect images and conceptions that they know not what to make of within, nor consequently how to bring out.

Montaigne, 'Of the Education of Children', *Essays*

One kind of criticism alone is worthy of respect. It says to the poet: This is what you willed to create, for this you were fated to will. It then proceeds to investigate the relation of the product to the producing will. All other criticism is of evil.

Friedrich Hebbel, *Tagebücher*

Danger is a good teacher, and makes apt scholars. So are disgrace, defeat, exposure to immediate scorn and laughter. There is no opportunity in such cases for self-delusion, no idling time away, no being off your guard (or you must take the consequences)— neither is there any room for humour or caprice or prejudice. If the Indian Juggler were to play tricks in throwing up the three case-knives, he would cut off his fingers. I can make a very bad antithesis without cutting off my fingers. The tact of style is more ambiguous than that of double-edged instruments.

William Hazlitt, 'The Indian Jugglers'

He who goes against the fashion is himself its slave.

Logan Pearsall Smith, *Afterthoughts*

I am all for the man who, with an average audience before him, uses all means of persuasion—stories, laughter, tears, and but so much of music as he can discover on the wings of words. I would even avoid the conversation of lovers of music, who would draw us into the impersonal land of sound and colour, and I would have no one write with a sonata in his memory.

William Butler Yeats, 'The Musician and the Orator'
The Cutting of an Agate

'Your study seems to be a large room.'

'No. Small. I prefer working in a small room. We have a family joke about it: "In a small room thoughts grow great; in a great room thoughts grow small." '

The question arose whether it was best to keep regular working hours.

'I know it is supposed to be a good rule,' he conceded, 'but I never could accomplish my best work that way. It is no doubt excellent for scientific men, but'—he quoted Goethe's dictum to Eckermann— ' "My counsel is to force nothing and rather to trifle and sleep away all unproductive days and hours, than on such days to compose something that will afterwards give no pleasure." '

Lucien Price, 'Portrait of Sibelius'
We Northmen

To write weekly, to write daily, to write shortly, to write for busy people catching trains in the morning or for tired people coming home in the evening, is a heartbreaking task for men who know good writing from bad. They do it, but instinctively draw out of harm's way anything precious that might be damaged by contact with the public, or anything sharp that might irritate its skin.

Virginia Woolf, 'The Modern Essay'
The Common Reader

So far from the position holding true, that great wit (or genius, in our modern way of speaking) has a necessary alliance with insanity, the greatest wits, on the contrary, will ever be found to be the sanest writers. It is impossible for the mind to conceive a mad Shakespeare. The greatness of wit, by which the poetic talent is here chiefly understood, manifests itself in the admirable balance of all faculties. Madness is the disproportionate straining or excess of any one of them. . . . The ground of the mistake is, that men, finding in the raptures of the higher poetry a condition of exaltation to which they have no parallel in their own experience, besides the spurious resemblance of it in dreams and fevers, impute a state of dreaminess and fever to the poets. But the true poet dreams being awake. He is not possessed by his subject, but has dominion over it.

Charles Lamb, 'The Sanity of True Genius'
Last Essays of Elia

People do not deserve to have good writing, they are so pleased with bad. In these sentences you show me, I can find no beauty, for I see death in every clause and every word. There is a fossil or a mummy character which pervades this book. I like gardens and nurseries. Give me initiative, spermatic, prophesying, man-making words.

R. W. Emerson, *Journals*

Thou wert never in more fair way to be cozened, than in this age, in poetry; wherein antics to run away from nature, and be afraid of her, is the only point of art that tickles the spectators. For they commend writers, as they do fencers or wrestlers; who, if they come in robustiously, and put for it with a great deal of violence, are received for the braver fellows. I deny not, but that these men, who always seek to do more than enough, may some time happen on something that is good, and great, but very seldom. I give thee this warning, that there is a great difference between these, that utter all they can, however unfitly; and those that use election and a mean. For it is only the disease of the unskilful, to think rude things greater than polished; or scattered more numerous than composed.

Ben Jonson, *The Alchemist*

The mind is like a bow, the stronger by being unbent. But the temper in spirits is all, when to commend a man's wit, when to favor it. I have known a man vehement on both sides, that knew no mean, either to intermit his studies or call upon them again. When he hath set himself to writing he would join night to day, press upon himself without release, not minding it till he fainted; and when he left off, resolve himself into all sports and looseness again, that it was almost a despair to draw him to his book; but once he got to it, he grew stronger and more earnest by the ease.

Ben Jonson, *Timber: or Discoveries*

My difficulty proceeds from the fact that, for each chapter, I must make a fresh start. Never profit from gathered momentum—such is the rule of my game.   André Gide, *Journals*

There never has been a story yet which has not back-watered at a state of semi-completion. It is a form of cowardice which overwhelms me, making me want to turn and run, making me wonder why I ever thought the idea was any good at all. To remember that this is a phase—not an irreparable state of mind—ought to help me to get over the mood quickly with each story.

Ruth Blodgett, Unpublished Notebooks

It is most wise not to worry too much about the intermissions (*temps d'arrêt*) in one's work. They air the subject and infuse it with life.

André Gide, *Journals*

Dec. 8. I thought and thought this morning but not to much avail. I can't think why, but my wit seems to be nearly deserting me when I want to get down to earth. I am all right—sky-high. And even in my brain, in my head, I can think and act and write wonders; but the moment I really try to put them down I fail miserably.

Katherine Mansfield, *Journals*

We are never satisfied with the maturity of those whom we have admired in boyhood; and, because we have seen their whole circle—even the most successful life is a segment—we remain to the end their harshest critics. One old school-fellow of mine will never believe that I have fulfilled the promise of some rough unscannable verses that I wrote before I was eighteen. Does any imaginative man find in maturity the admiration that his first half-inarticulate years roused in some little circle; and is not the first success the greatest?

William Butler Yeats, 'The Trembling of the Veil'
Autobiographies

Not on sad Stygian shore, nor in clear sheen
Of far Elysian plain, shall we meet those
Among the dead whose pupils we have been,
Nor those great shades whom we have held as foes;

No meadow of asphodel our feet shall tread,
Nor shall we look each other in the face
To love or hate each other being dead,
Hoping some praise, or fearing some disgrace.

We shall not argue, saying 'T'was thus,' or 'thus,'
Our argument's whole drift we shall forget;
Who's right, who's wrong, 'twill all be one to us;
We shall not even know that we have met.

Yet meet we shall, and part, and meet again,
Where dead men meet, on lips of living men.

Samuel Butler, *Notebooks*

He could see, in a few pages, what Joyce was doing; it was thrilling, but it was something to consider

by patient intuition, not to palaver and write papers
about. There is no harm in reading any number of
unimportant books for pastime, but the significant
books must be taken cautiously. You don't want
them to get in the way of what may perhaps be
growing and brooding in yourself, taking its own
time.   Christopher Morley, *John Mistletoe*

He punctuated after the manner of the seventeenth
century and was always ready to spend an hour dis-
cussing the exact use of the colon. 'One should use
a colon where other people use a semi-colon, a semi-
colon where other people use a comma', was, I think,
but a condescension to my ignorance, for the matter
was plainly beset with many difficulties.

William Butler Yeats, 'The Tragic Veil'
Autobiographies

A good style in literature, if closely examined,
will be seen to consist in a constant succession of tiny
surprises.   Ford Madox Ford

Style is the man. Style, too, is autobiography. If
the author withholds his face, we can learn something about him from the mask behind which he
has chosen to conceal himself.   John Cournos

What I propose is to dispense with a style. Let us
have style instead of a style. No one, as a matter of
fact, gets rid of a certain gait, which, to the eye of
the delicate observer, gives a family likeness to all

his works. But let us carry our style next the skin instead of wearing it on our sleeve; let us bother about having good stuff to our coat rather than about putting smart patterns on it.

Jean Cocteau, *Le Secret Professionel*

I cannot grasp the contemporary notion that the traditional virtues of style are incompatible with a poetry of modern subject matter; it appears to rest on the fallacy of expressive form, the notion that the form of the poem should express the matter. This fallacy results in the writing of chaotic poetry about the traffic; of loose poetry about our sprawling nation; of semi-conscious poetry about our semi-conscious states. But the matter of poetry is and always has been chaotic; it is raw nature. To let the form of the poem succumb to its matter is and always will be the destruction of poetry and may be the destruction of intelligence. Poetry is form; its constituents are thought and feeling as they are embedded in language; and though form cannot be wholly reduced to principles, there are certain principles which it can not violate.

Yvor Winters, *Before Disaster*

In life courtesy and self-possession, and in the arts style, are the sensible impressions of the free mind, for both arise out of a deliberate shaping of all things, and from never being swept away, whatever the emotion, into confusion or dulness.

William Butler Yeats, 'Poetry and Tradition'
The Cutting of an Agate

I believe in a wild profusion of imagery if need be, so that there be structure underneath and impressive cogency in what is said.

William Rose Benét, 'Round About Parnassus'

And the unwillingness to make imaginative effort is the prime cause of almost all decay of art. It is the caterer, the man whose business it is to provide enjoyment with the very minimum of effort, who is in matters of art the real assassin.

Gilbert Murray, *Religio Grammaticus*

But this I know: the writer who possesses the creative gift owns something of which he is not always master—something that, at times, strangely wills and works for itself. He may lay down rules and devise principles, and to rules and principles it will perhaps for years lie in subjection; and then, haply without any warning or revolt, there comes a time when it will no longer consent to 'harrow the valleys, or be bound with a band in the furrow'—when 'it laughs at the multitude of the city, and regards not the crying of the driver'—when, refusing absolutely to make ropes out of sea-sand any longer, it sets to work on statue-hewing, and you have a Pluto or a Jove, a Tisiphone or a Psyche, a Mermaid or a Madonna, as Fate or Inspiration direct. Be the work grim or glorious, dread or divine, you have little choice left but quiescent adoption. As for you—the nominal artist—your share in it has been to work passively under dictates you neither delivered nor could question—that would not be uttered at your

prayer, nor suppressed nor changed at your caprice.
If the result be attractive, the World will praise you,
who little deserve praise; if it be repulsive, the same
World will blame you, who almost as little deserve
blame.

Charlotte Brontë, Preface to *Wuthering Heights*

At least six distinctive senses of the word 'imagination' are still current in critical discussion. . . .

(i) The reproduction of vivid images, usually
visual images . . . is the commonest and least interesting thing which is referred to by imagination.

(ii) The use of figurative language is frequently
all that is meant. People who naturally employ metaphor and simile, especially when it is of an unusual
kind, are said to have imagination.

(iii) A narrower sense is that in which sympathetic reproducing of other people's states of mind,
particularly their emotional states, is what is meant.
'You haven't enough imagination,' the dramatist
says to the critic who thinks that his persons behave
unnaturally.

(iv) Inventiveness, the bringing together of elements which are not ordinarily connected, is another
sense. According to this Edison is said to have possessed imagination, and any fantastic romance will
show it in excelsis. Although this comes nearer to a
sense in which value is implied, it is still too general.
The lunatic will beat any of us at combining odd
ideas.

(v) Next we have that kind of relevant connection of things ordinarily thought of as disparate which is exemplified in scientific imagination. This is the ordering of experience in definite ways and for a definite end or purpose, not necessarily deliberate and conscious, but limited to a given field of phenomena. The technical triumphs of the arts are instances of this kind of imagination.

(vi) 'That synthetic and magical power, to which we have exclusively appropriated the name of imagination . . . reveals itself in the balance or reconciliation of opposite or discordant qualities . . . the sense of novelty and freshness, with old and familiar objects; a more than usual state of emotion, with more than usual order; judgment ever awake and self-possession with enthusiasm and feeling profound or vehement.' 'The sense of musical delight . . . with the power of reducing multitude into unity of effect, and modifying a series of thoughts by some one predominant thought or feeling.'— Coleridge.

I. A. Richards, 'The Imagination'
Principles of Literary Criticism

The more extensive your acquaintance is with the works of those who have excelled, the more extensive will be your powers of invention, and what may appear still more like a paradox, the more original will be your composition.

Sir Joshua Reynolds,
Discourse to the Royal Academy

Experience is never limited, and it is never complete; it is an immense sensibility, a kind of huge spider web of the finest silken threads suspended in the chamber of consciousness, and catching every air-borne particle in its tissues. It is the very atmosphere of the mind; and when the mind is imaginative—much more when it happens to be that of a man of genius—it takes to itself the faintest hints of life, it converts the very pulse of the air into revelations.

Henry James, 'The Art of Fiction'
Partial Portraits

It is to the inventive imagination that we look for deliverance from every other misfortune as from the desolation of a flat Hellenic perfection of style. . . . The true value is that peculiarity which gives an object a character by itself. . . . The imagination goes from one thing to another. Given many things of nearly totally divergent natures, but possessing one-thousandth part of a quality in common, provided that be new, distinguished, these things belong in an imaginative category and not in a gross natural array. . . . But the thing that stands eternally in the way of really good writing is always one: the virtual impossibility of lifting to the imagination those things which lie under the direct scrutiny of the senses, close to the nose.

By the brokenness of his composition the poet makes himself a master of a certain weapon which he could possess himself of in no other way. The speed of the emotions is sometimes such that . . .

many matters are touched but not held, more often broken by the contact. . . . Thus a poem is tough by no quality it borrows from a logical recital of events nor from the events themselves but solely from the attenuated power which draws perhaps many broken things into a dance giving them thus full being.

William Carlos Williams, *Kora in Hell*

In every human being there is the artist, and whatever his activity, he has an equal chance with any to express the result of his growth and his contact with life . . . I don't believe any real artist cares whether what he does is 'art' or not. Who, after all, knows what is art? I think the real artists are too busy with just being and growing and acting (on canvas or however) like themselves, to worry about the end. This end is what it will be. The object is intense living, fulfilment, the great happiness in creation.   Robert Henri, *The Art Spirit*

Art lives upon discussion, upon experiment, upon curiosity, upon variety of attempt, upon the exchange of views and the comparison of standpoints; and there is a presumption that those times when no one has anything particular to say about it, and has no reason to give for practice or preference, though they may be times of honour, are not time of development—are times, possibly, even of a little dulness.

Henry James, 'The Art of Fiction'
Partial Portraits

Some may know what they seek in school and
  church,
And why they seek it there; for what I search
I must go measuring stone walls, perch on perch;

Sure that though not a star of death and birth,
So not to be compared, perhaps, in worth
To such resorts of life as Mars and Earth,

Though not, I say, a star of death and sin,
It yet has poles, and only needs a spin
To show its worldly nature and begin

To chafe and shuffle in my calloused palm
And run off in strange tangents with my arm
As fish do with the line in first alarm.

Such as it is, it promises the prize
Of the one world complete in any size
That I am like to compass, fool or wise.

> Robert Frost, 'Star in a Stone-Boat'
> *New Hampshire*

When I was young, I painted as my nature com-
pelled me to. Today I do so still, only then it seemed
to give me more pleasure. Two uncompleted sketch-
es did me more good then than all the recommenda-
tions of a whole academy. But one doesn't always
stay young. What concerned me was gradually to
acquire understanding of what I was doing. With
every picture in which I freed myself I came nearer
to myself. Matisse, *Notebooks*

Time extracts various values from a painter's work. When these values are exhausted the pictures are forgotten, and the more a picture has to give, the greater it is. Matisse, *Notebooks*

Life has at last been perfectly formed and measured to man's requirements; and in art man knows himself truly the master of his existence. It is this sense of mastery which gives man that raised and delighted consciousness of self which art provokes.
Lascelles Abercrombie, *Study of Thomas Hardy*

Of human activities, writing poetry is one of the least revolutionary. The states of being a rentier, a capitalist, contribute their bits to the revolution: they actively crumble. But the writing of a poem in itself solves the poem's problem. Separate poems are separate and complete and ideal worlds. . . . A work of art cannot reach out into everyday life and tell us whom to vote for and what kind of factories to build, because injunctions how to act in a world that has nothing to do with the poem destroy the poem's unity.
Stephen Spender, *Poetry and Revolution*

A great part of our racial knowledge of our lives and our earth and our destiny upon that earth has come in all ages from the intuitive and emotional perception of great poets. The poet works with those dimensions of invisibility which exist at the opposite extreme from the microscopic dimensions which concern the scientist. He works with the over-obvious, the too-apparent, the phenomena which men cannot see because they are so close the vision blurs, the phenomena which approach the seeing eye so near that they become sometimes the seeing eye itself. It is for this reason that the true perceptions of the poet have such an overwhelming and instantaneous feel of truth. They require no demonstration because they were always true. They were merely never 'seen' before. The poet, with the adjustment of a phrase, with the contrast of an image, with the rhythm of a line, has fixed a focus which all the talk and all the staring of the world has been unable to fix before him.

Archibald MacLeish, 'The Poetry of Karl Marx'

Man, as the savage first conceived him, man, as the mind of science still affirms, is not the center of the world he lives in, but merely one of her myriad products, more conscious than the rest and more perplexed. . . . He may cower before it like a savage, study it impartially for what it is, like the man of science; it remains in the end, as in the beginning, something alien and inhuman, often destructive of his hopes. But a third way is open. He may construct, within the world as it is, a pattern of the world as he would have it. This is the way of humanism, in philosophy, and in the arts.

Geoffrey Scott, *The Architecture of Humanism*

THE POET'S DIFFICULTIES

THE poet's difficulties are of two kinds, public and private, but it is the private difficulty which requires his unremitting care; his public problems are only an extension of them. Both rise from the nature of his position, from the inescapable fact that among men he is a poet, and must maintain himself in his place with honourable success. In neither predicament may he be caught off his guard. Since the spirit he is at such pains to discipline is the originator of his poems, the poet's work begins here, is carried on here all his life, and all but ends here. Only his written poems, his published books, are valid evidence of victory in the long, silent battle.

'A war-like, various, and tragical age is best to write of, but worst to write in,' said Abraham Cowley. The poet is fortunate who feels that he has been born in the right age, at a time he would have chosen if he had the choice; and more than fortunate if he is right about it. The seventeenth century was warlike and various, but not tragical, and the poets lived in the full of their time. Their writing was their life, as lusty, proud, dangerous, and golden a literature as any poet could wish to be part of. The nineteenth century was in many ways tragical, and in some various; the social and intellectual changes were profound. The eighteenth century was none of these things. 'Poetry did not rise spontaneously in their hearts, as true poetry should,' said A. E. Housman, 'and the result was that they wrote more verse. Either they had things to say, which is likely to be death to poetry; or they concentrated their attention upon form, which is fatal.' But the twentieth century, near its half, is all too certainly a good age to write of, being terribly and undeniably war-like, various, and tragical; but a bad age to write in. This the poet makes it his business to understand. On this map of history he must calculate his North, South, East, and West, and locate himself.

Always nearer than the shapes of history are the people who, though they do not know it, are making history, and who, though the poet does not know them, are his readers, his enemies, or his indifferent fellow-men. Too much quivering indignation has been spent on the cruelty of those who neglect poets. Millions in every generation can live well without poetry, and do; a few thousands cannot live without it, and sometimes a few hundred may be won from the larger number to the smaller. But the poet who does not persuade his millions, or even his hundreds, should blame himself. He has, however, more immediate difficulties with enemies and readers, since both respond in positive ways to his existence. The poet must know that many people object to his existence on the ground that he is lazy, unmanly, and exclusive. They feel that no poet earns his living legitimately, because he does not do the sort of work that can be watched for real results. They are uneasy about his preoccupation with words and feelings, because that seems to them the business of women; what they remember is a time when women lived gently and in idleness, sewing, singing, reading books; not a manly life. And they violently object to the suggestion that they do not understand, and could not appreciate, if it were explained, the fineness of the art of poetry. These three attitudes combine in the suspicion with which the poet is often regarded. It is an important part of the poet's work as poet to free himself of this suspicion, by refusing to confirm it in his actions, and by confidence in himself and his kind to keep himself unbewildered in his experience of it.

From the friendly part of the public the poet will receive such payment in money as he ever gets from poetry; ordinarily it is very little. 'Can you find some way of earning a decently liberal living,' asks Arthur Davison Ficke of a young poet, 'quite apart from your writing? Are you aware that poverty is a dark room, into which no sane man will voluntarily go? Do you know that the lovely fable of the poet's attic is a lie invented by rich people, and that lack of books and of diversion and of freedom is stunting to the soul?' And it is a hard but unavoidable fact that of twelve poets the last century called great, nine had the means to get a university education, and only one was not well-to-do. That one was John Keats. The son of an Athenian slave, said Sir Arthur Quiller-Couch, had as much hope as a poor poet in England of emancipation into that intellectual freedom of which great writings are born. But if the poet finds a 'decently liberal living' aside from his poetry, and writes his poetry also, the friendly intentions of the public are still dangerous. The poet must teach himself never to propitiate the public for the sake of its praise, or for the sake of its good company, or for more of its money than another more rigorous poet gets. He must not deliberately be in style. If he makes the style, yet keeps his independence, he has his reward. But he may not say what people want to hear him say, unless his inner forces are in accord with the outer forces. It is the hardest lesson the artist learns, but from failure in it there is no recovery, no second chance.

It is clear that these relations with the world, so precariously maintained and so vital a condition of success, come from the poet's character, and derive from that character whatever healthy endurance they are to show. Not to be second-rate, is the poet's most private prayer. Not to be less than great in spirit, less than excellent in technique, less than adequate in energy for the completion of every poem undertaken. And although without help and against external odds this level has been achieved, there is no real necessity for such loneliness in self-discipline, for there are always excellent examples. The behaviour of false poets, of whom there are five or ten times as many as there are true poets, will warn him in one direction. The less obvious behaviour of the good poets will guide him in the other. Self-study is constantly illuminated by the study of excellent example. The young poet works under a bright blessing who has a great living poet for friend, to whom he may now and then show his work, and with whom he may turn the many sides of thought to the light of day for examination. Literal apprenticeship, though right cases were rare, might be worth a revival. But the poet at work in self-perfection will learn from such sources however near or far. 'His books are indeed a principal source,' wrote Malcolm Cowley, 'but there is also to be considered his career, the point from which it started, the direction in which it seems to be moving. There is his personality as revealed in chance interviews or caricatured in gossip; there are the values he assigns to other writers; and there is the value placed on himself by his younger colleagues.'

From all this the poet at the beginning of his career chooses what he needs, and rejects what he knows is not good for him. Dramatic or amusing as it sometimes seems, the young poet will avoid displays of the artistic temperament, for he will learn that it is merely a way of describing everything that hinders the artist in producing. Wide acquaintanceship among literary men, though it comes as an inevitable and welcome reward for literary success, presents complex difficulties. Few poets are charitable to one another; the prize they are all after is too great, and the competition too ruthless, to make it safe to come unarmed and unready into such gatherings. Oscar Wilde once observed that the basis of literary friendship is mixing the poisoned bowl. And there are the dinners and the luncheons, the celebrations, the poetry groups of all kinds, with which society, though with eager good intention, cripples and silences the poet. He must be very shrewd in his choices, and very patient in his refusals. He needs all his strength for poetry; he is extraordinarily generous if he can share it with the world in any other forms.

The time comes when the poet is in trouble of a sort that cannot be helped by his friends or his friendly public. It is difficult enough to write a poem—it is the one difficulty we may assume without discussion—but to have no poem to write is worst of all. Then only the strength the poet has cherished within can be called upon: his sincerity, his invention, his spiritual richness. Then he is thankful if he has not given part of himself away; and if he has, he is lost. Then the poets he admires do him no good. Then the meetings of poetry groups, the public readings, the luncheons to honour the visiting writer, are elaborate torture. It is the most private and the most desperate of the poet's difficulties, and an experience known to all men of imagination. It is against this time almost as much as for the bright furious hours of creation that he has been preparing himself. 'You know the Black Thought, Gentlemen?' asked Rudyard Kipling. 'It possesses some men in the dead of night; some when they are setting their palettes; some when they are stropping their razors; but only the very young, the very sound, the very single, are exempt.'

Young the poet may always be, if he has taught

himself to stay awake and stay alive, so that as his poetry grows it moves from vigour to new vigour. If he has resisted the enemy within and without, parrying even unsuspected difficulties with skill, then no one knows better than himself his soundness. His singleness is his secret. We may not invade that. But we can read the poems in his books.

'NO ROYAL ROAD'

The notion that poetry, and sonnets in particular, are written only by the mild-mannered, and persons in precarious health, requires to be dispelled. As a fact, great poets are not only the sanest people in the world, but physically and temperamentally the toughest.

        T. W. H. Crosland, *The English Sonnet*

Dear N——

It is a little hard to comply with your request and give you sensible advice on the subject. But I will try. Let me first ask you a series of questions.

Are you willing to work for many years without the slightest recognition? Are you strong enough to turn your back on all the cliques and schools of the hour, and devote yourself to principles of poetic composition that have not changed since the days of David the Psalmist? Would you rather write poetry than have all the kingdoms of the earth at your feet?

Are you strong enough to bear the dislike of the mob? Are you individual enough to go your own way, no matter what prudent counsel advises an opposite course?

Have you a real desire to explore the last depths of your emotions? Are you aware that those emotions are of no interest to anybody, except in so far as you give them beautiful and dignified expression?

Can you study endlessly the great masters of the past? Can you learn the lesson of their method—not merely of their manner—and borrow from them nothing except their power to express the passion of the individual heart? Can you refrain from copying them? Can you refrain from being 'modern'?

Can you find some way of earning a decently liberal living, quite apart from your writing? Are you aware that poverty is a dark room, into which no sane man will voluntarily go? Do you know that the lovely fable of the poet's attic is a lie invented by rich people, and that lack of books and of diversion and of freedom is stunting to the soul? Are you prepared, I repeat, to earn a decent living quite apart from your poetry?

If you can honestly answer all these questions in the affirmative—then, I would say to you: 'Go on! I wish you well! Maybe your great hopes will come true.'

Arthur Davison Ficke, 'Letter to a Poet'

Wanting to be a poet may be only an indication that you are afraid to take hold of life as most people live it. You may be using that ambition as a convenient lever to pry you loose from conditions of living that you hate, a piece of personal adornment to compensate for the fact that you do not seem especially desirable to others. In such cases, with a change of circumstances, your ambition to write will die. Another flaw in your purpose in life may lie in wanting to be a certain kind of person instead of wanting to do a certain kind of thing—to be a poet rather than to write poetry. That is like choosing a job for the uniform. Even loving poetry may mean only that you like to read it, not write it.

Anonymous

Write then, now that you are young, nonsense by the ream. Be silly, be sentimental, imitate Shelley, imitate Samuel Smiles; give the rein to every impulse; commit every fault of style, grammar, taste, and syntax; pour out; tumble over; loose anger, love, satire, in whatever words you can catch, coerce or create, in whatever metre, prose, poetry, or gibberish that comes to hand. But if you publish, your freedom will be checked; you will be thinking what people will say; you will write for others when you ought to be writing for yourself. And what point can there be in curbing the wild torrent of spontaneous nonsense which is now, for a few years only, your divine gift in order to publish prim little books of experimental verses? To make money? That, we both know, is out of the question. To get criticism? But your friends will pepper your manuscripts with

far more serious and searching criticism than you
will get from the reviewers. As for fame, look I im-
plore you at famous people; see how the waters of
dulness spread around them as they enter; observe
their pomposity, the prophetic airs; reflect that the
greatest poets were anonymous; think how Shakespeare cared nothing for fame; how Donne tossed his
poems into the waste-paper basket; write an essay
giving a single instance of any modern English
writer who has survived the desciples and admirers,
the autograph hunters and the interviewers, the dinners and the luncheons, the celebrations and the
commemorations with which English society so
effectively stops the mouths of its singers and silences
their songs.

Virginia Woolf, *A Letter to a Young Poet*

'But it's poetry!' That was an exclamation never
heard before this mechanical age, unless with pleas-
urable anticipation.   Henry S. Canby

Holding the Pose:—At times when second-rate
artists are doing their best work they can hardly
be distinguished from the truly great. Yet what
they always lack is the ability to keep themselves
at the required height for a sufficient length of time.
Precisely at those moments when the last extraordinary straining of all their energies would be necessary, they are fated to sink into the paltry, the trivial,
or the absurd.

Arthur Schnitzler, 'Work and Echo'

Understand that you can have in your writing no qualities which you do not honestly entertain in yourself. Understand that you cannot keep out of your writing the indication of the evil or shallowness you entertain in yourself. If you love to have a servant stand behind your chair at dinner, it will appear in your writing; if you possess a vile opinion of women, or if you begrudge anything, or doubt immortality, these will appear by what you leave unsaid more than by what you say. There is no trick or cunning by which you can have in your writing that which you do not possess in yourself.

Walt Whitman, Memoranda for *Leaves of Grass*

But the end of contemplating the eternal beauties, and doing nothing to yoke them with time, is smugness, and stagnation, and sterility.

Rebecca West, *Harriet Hume*

Temperament:—When we speak of the artistic temperament we are usually referring to the sum quantities which hinder the artist in producing.

Arthur Schnitzler, 'Work and Echo'

No matter how the poet may sweat and fast to produce his ode, the chances are that in the poem he will visualize himself as reclining somewhere on a mossy bank beside a running brook. Sir Thomas Wyatt celebrated his bed as 'the body's ease' and 'quieter of the mind'. Few have been so frank as Wordsworth, who admits lying in vacant as well as pensive mood, but many have professed with Coleridge that they were fain to

> dream away the entrusted hours
> On rose-leaf beds, pampering the coward heart
> With feelings all too delicate for use.

Keats, 'on Skiddaw's mount lay supine, midway th' ascent.' Is it any wonder, then, that the reader, remembering in addition that Coleridge composed 'Kubla Khan' while asleep in a chair, considers the writing of poetry a lazy man's occupation? The public, not unreasonably, perhaps, is prone to take their words literally. The 'pernicious nonsense' of the 'essential laziness' of poets is, sad to say, a pleasant fiction largely of their own invention.

Raymond F. Howes

> We make ourselves a place apart
>   Behind light words that tease and flout,
> But oh, the agitated heart
>   Till someone find us really out.
>   Robert Frost, 'Revelation', *A Boy's Will*

The world is a perpetual caricature of itself; at every moment it is the mockery and contradiction of what it is pretending to be. But as it nevertheless intends all the time to be something different and highly dignified, at the next moment it corrects and checks and tries to cover up the absurd thing it was; so that a conventional world, a world of masks, is superimposed on the reality, and passes in every sphere of human interest for the reality itself. Humour is the perception of this illusion, whilst the convention continues to be maintained, as if we had not observed its absurdity.

George Santayana, *Soliloquies in England*

People who read books without writing them are likely to form a simple picture of any celebrated author. He is John X or Jonathan Y, the man who wrote such a fascinating novel about Paris, about divorce, about the Georgia crackers—the man who drinks, the man who ran off with the doctor's wife— the bald-headed man who lectured to the Wednesday Club. But to writers, especially to young writers in search of guidance, the established author presents a much more complicated image, and one that is assembled from many sources. His books are indeed a principal source, but there is also to be considered his career, the point from which it started, the direction in which it seems to be moving. There is his personality as revealed in chance interviews or caricatured in gossip; there are the values he assigns to other writers; and there is the value placed on himself by his younger colleagues in those kitchen or barroom gatherings at which they pass judgement with the harsh finality of a Supreme Court—John X has got the real stuff, they say, but Jonathan Y is terrible—and they bring forward evidence to support these verdicts. The evidence is mulled over, all the details are fitted together like the pieces of a jigsaw puzzle, until they begin to form a picture, vague and broken at first, then growing more distinct as the years pass by: the X or Y picture, the James Joyce, Paul Valéry, or T. S. Eliot picture. But it is not so much a picture when completed: it is rather a map or diagram which the apprentice will use in planning his own career.

Malcolm Cowley, *Exile's Return*

Bad literature justifies itself by treating more important matters than good writers have the courage to touch upon; violent sentiments, adultery, ostracism, guilt, and redemption.

Glenway Wescott, 'A Guilty Woman'
Goodbye Wisconsin

The miserable man may think well and express himself with great vehemence, but he cannot make beautiful things, for Aphrodite never rises from any but a tide of joy.　　　William Butler Yeats

Men are free when they are in a living homeland, not when they are straying and breaking away. Men are free when they are obeying some deep, inward voice of religious belief. Men are free when they belong to a living, organic believing community, active in fulfilling some unfulfilled, perhaps unrealized purpose. Not when they are escaping to some wild west. The most unfree souls go west, and shout of freedom. Men are freest when they are most unconscious of freedom. The shout is a rattling of chains, always was.　　　D. H. Lawrence,
Studies in Classic American Literature

It was Chrysis' theory of life that all human beings —save a few who seemed to possess some secret from the gods—merely endured the slow misery of existence, hiding as best they could their consternation that life had no wonderful surprises after all and that its most difficult burden was the incommunicability of love.

Thornton Wilder, *Woman of Andros*

We grow neither better nor worse as we get old, but more like ourselves.

May Lamberton Becker, 'The Reader's Guide'

Thoreau's quality is very penetrating and contagious; reading him is like eating onions—one must look out or the flavour will reach his own page. But my current is as strong in my channel as Thoreau's in his.   John Burroughs, *Journal*

People do not ask painters to go places and paint pictures for nothing, but they are forever trying to graft entertainment off of poets.   Don Marquis

They that write of poisons, and of creatures naturally disposed to the ruin of man, do as well mention the flea as the viper, because the flea, though he kill none, he does all the harm he can.

John Donne, 'Devotions'

Nothing in our age, I have observed, is more preposterous, than the running judgements upon Poetry, and Poets; when we shall hear those things commended, and cry'd up for the best writings, which a man would scarce vouchsafe to wrap any wholesome drug in; he would never light his tobacco with them. And those men almost named for Miracles, who are not yet so vile, that if a man should go about to examine and correct them, he must make all they have done but one blot. Their good is so entangled with their bad, as forcibly one must draw on the others death with it.

> Ben Jonson, *Timber: or Discoveries*

The basis of literary friendships is mixing the poisoned bowl.   Oscar Wilde

Noise is the most impertinent of all forms of interruption. It is not only an interruption, but a disruption of thought. Of course, where there is nothing to interrupt, noise will not be so particularly painful.

> Schopenhauer, *Studies in Pessimism*

There is nothing worse for our trade than to be in
   style:
He that goes naked goes farther at last than another:
Wrap the bard in a flag or a school and they'll jimmy
   his
Door down and be thick in his bed—for a month:

(Who recalls the address now of the Imagists?)
But the naked man has always his own nakedness:
People remember him forever his live limbs:

> Archibald MacLeish,
> 'Invocation to the Social Muse', *Poems* 1924-1933

What American literature needs is not more poets (we could dispense with most of those already writing), but mature poets who are willing to devote their whole time to the most difficult of arts.

Malcolm Cowley, 'The Business of Being a Poet'

Nine-tenths of the best poetry in the world has been written by poets less than thirty-five years old; a great deal more than half of it has been written by poets under twenty-five. One always associates poetry with youth, for it deals chiefly with ideas that are peculiar to youth, and its terminology is quite as youthful as its contents. When one hears of a poet past thirty-five, he seems somewhat unnatural and a trifle obscene; it is as if one encountered a graying man who still played Chopin waltzes and believed in elective affinities.

H. L. Mencken, 'The Poet and His Art'
Prejudices, 3d Series

He hopes to live by writing poems, and yet he has no assurance that his poems will be accepted by magazines. If they happen to be accepted, he has no assurance that they will be regarded as anything else than a free contribution to the cause of letters. Let us assume, however, that he is paid for his work at the rate of fifty cents a line, and that being exceptionally prolific he can produce the equivalent of eight or nine sonnets every month. In this case, granting that all his poems are printed, he will be earning

about $14 a week—approximately as much as the
striking mill-hands in North Carolina.

    Malcolm Cowley, 'The Business of Being a Poet'

It is felt, pretty widely, that poetry is an effeminate
business, and that poets are not 'men'. When a poet
somehow becomes news, the papers are at pains to
state that he wears his hair short, enjoys his beer, and
attends boxing matches.

    L. A. G. Strong, *Common Sense About Poetry*

> I had rather hear a brazen canstick turned
> Or a dry wheel grate on the axle-tree;
> And that would set my teeth nothing on edge,
> Nothing so much as mincing poetry.
>
>   Shakespeare, *Henry IV*

I have been breaking silence these twenty-three
years and have hardly made a rent in it.

    H. D. Thoreau, *Journals*

There are also the false poets, the bad poets, who
rush about, reading their stuff to anyone who will
listen: eager for any audience, however unskilled,
and vexing even strangers in their indecent haste to
expose their writings. The true poet does not behave
in this fashion; and therefore, if the ordinary reader
has ever been subjected to this kind of treatment, it
will have been one of these preposterous asses, who
thereby get a bad name for the craft they are aping.

    L. A. G. Strong, *Common Sense About Poetry*

No matter how sagacious or how revered the teacher, at some point you will find yourself beginning to diverge from him. For sooner or later, every individual has to fall back on that residual and personal parcel of conviction which is true for himself alone.   Christopher Morley, *Inward Ho!*

> By all means use sometimes to be alone.
> Salute thyself: see what thy soul doth wear.
> Dare to look in thy chest; for 'tis thine own;
> And tumble up and down what thou find'st there.
> Who cannot rest till he good fellows find,
> He breaks up house, turns out of doors his mind.
>   George Herbert, 'The Church Porch'

I can no longer expect to be revisited by the continuous excitement under which in the early months of 1895 I wrote the greater part of my other book.
        A. E. Housman, Preface to *Last Poems*

Success is, indeed, as Trollope says somewhere, a necessary poison; but they are fortunate, he wisely adds, to whom it comes late in life and in small doses . . . the number of miscarriages of talent, the rate of infant mortality among gifts of promise, seems to be ever increasing. And indeed, with all the advertisement and premature publicity of our time, where can we hope to find that leisurely ripening of talent in the shade of obscurity, that slow development by experiment and failure, by which it can best be mellowed and matured?   Logan Pearsall Smith,
'The Prospects of Literature'

I doubt if Emerson could trundle a wheelbarrow through the streets, because it would be out of character. One needs to have a comprehensive character.

H. D. Thoreau, *Journals*

When you meet, in the flesh, a writer whose work has seemed to you to have tragic force, you are apt to feel that, face to face and talking with him, you are, in essentials, further removed from him than you were when you only read his books. . . . Compared with that self-revealer, the man before you seems like a creature withdrawn into a shell. Between you and him there has now arisen the estranging film of defensive reticence which separates nearly all of us from our friends.

C. E. Montague, 'The Delights of Tragedy'
A Writer's Notes on His Trade

The conversation of authors is not so good as might be imagined: but, such as it is (and with rare exceptions) it is better than any other. The proof of which is, that when you are used to it, you cannot put up with any other.

William Hazlitt, 'On the Conversation of Authors'

Where the poet of the past was glad to share and quick to express the passions and foibles of those about him, the poet of today is proud only of his differences. It is no longer the self who desires a closer connection with and 'a greater knowledge of human nature'; it is, as Virginia Woolf wrote, 'a self that sits alone in a room at night with the blinds drawn . . . much less interested in what we have in common than what he has apart'. In short, the poet, for all his volubility, no longer believes in his high purpose, nor in himself. He seeks to charm or pique or entertain; he cannot exalt. He no longer delights in the passionate 'goings-on of the Universe' nor is he 'habitually impelled to create them' for the act of creation is an act of faith, and he has no faith in them. He does not really believe—and I may as well come out with the stilted and inevitable phrase—in the destiny of man.

Louis Untermeyer, ' "Poets to Come!" '
Play in Poetry

Have patience and indulgence toward the people, take off your hat to nothing known or unknown, or to any man or number of men, go freely with powerful uneducated persons.

Walt Whitman, Preface to *Leaves of Grass*

There's a free masonry among the dull by which they recognize and are sociable with the dull, as surely as a correspondent tact in men of genius.

R. W. Emerson, *Journals*

Detestable is the society of mere literary men.

Emmanuel Kant

Let us honour if we can
The vertical man
Though we value none
But the horizontal one.

W. H. Auden, Invocation to *Poems*

Somebody with whom I was talking cried: 'They are all only poetical persons—not poets. Who will be reading them a century hence?' To which I answered: 'There are so many of them that, a century hence, they may appear a kind of Composite Poet; there may be 500 excellent poems proceeding from 100 poets mostly not so very great, but well worth remembering a century hence.'

> Harold Monro,
> Preface to *Twentieth Century Poetry*

Rousseau's children are now forgotten
And he might be forgotten, too,
If he had not sent them to an orphan asylum
To free himself for the writing of books.
But, oh, to be remembered
For deserting your children
For the sake of learning the violin
And not learn it.

> Edgar Lee Masters, *The New Spoon River*

Nothing in literature is so perishable as eccentricity, with regard to which each generation has its own requirements and its own standard of taste; and the critic who urges contemporary poets to make their work as individual as possible is deliberately inviting them to build their structures on sand instead of rock.

> Edmond Holmes, *What is Poetry?*

All one's work might have been better done; but this is the sort of reflection a worker must put aside courageously if he doesn't want every one of his compositions to remain forever a private vision, an evanescent reverie.

Joseph Conrad, *Notes on My Books*

'Tis not every day that I
Fitted am to prophesy:
No, but when the Spirit fills
The fantastick Pannicles:
Full of fier; then I write
As the Godhead doth indite.
Thus inraged, my lines are hurl'd,
Like the Sybells, through the world.
Look how next the holy fier
Either slakes, or doth retire;
So the Fancie cools, till when
That brave Spirit comes again.

Robert Herrick, 'Not Every Day Fit for Verse'
Hesperides

A long poem was a new departure for him. He felt that it was time for him to make an attempt, but he dreaded it as well. I do not suppose that anyone not a poet can realize the agony of creating a poem. Every nerve, even every muscle, seems strained to the breaking point. The poem will not be denied, to refuse to write it would be a greater torture. It tears its way out of the brain, splintering and breaking its passage, and leaves that organ in the state of a jellyfish when the task is done. And yet to have no poem to write is the worst state of all.

Amy Lowell, *John Keats*

To be so lighthearted
What pain was left behind;
What fetters fallen gave them
Unto this airy mind.
     Æ (George Russell), 'The Gay', *Vale*

During periods of trouble the artist has only three
things which may vouch for him: his sincerity, his
spiritual richness, or his imagination.
                    Benjamin Crémieux,
          'Inquiétude et Réconstruction'

The crowd was always near; he ran to it
Glad to forget a moment how this wrong
Done to himself was eating bit by bit
The delicate food he should have saved for song.
Stuffing his ears, he talked to everybody:
The smart, the lazy, the polite, the shoddy.
                         Harrison Dowd

Like all artists, Byron and Shelley wrote in order
to console themselves for not living, and a man of
action appeared to them as an enviable phenomenon.
                    André Maurois, *Ariel*

I was in one of those disillusioned moods which
come to writers bankrupt of ideas, bankrupt of confidence, a prey to that recurrent despair, the struggle
which makes the profession of the pen 'a manly one.'
My eyes wandering over that fine countryside took
in the loveliness thereof with the profound discon-

tent of one who, seeing beauty, feels that he cannot render it.

> John Galsworthy, 'A Strange Thing'
> *Tatterdemalion*

A second chance—that's the delusion. There never was to be one. We work in the dark—we do what we can—we give what we have. Our doubt is our passion, and our passion is our task. The rest is the madness of art.

> Henry James, *The Middle Years*

The poet must always prefer the community where the perfected minds express the people, to a community that is vainly seeking to copy perfected minds.

> William Butler Yeats, 'The Galway Plains'
> *Ideas of Good and Evil*

The truth to be driven home is not that the poet is important. The truth to be driven home is that the poet is important only so long as he acts as poet. The intuitions of the poet are valid and may be accepted only because his loyalty is to his art, because his sole test of the acceptability of a word or a phrase or a poem is the test of his art and not the test of his politics or his social indignation.

> Archibald MacLeish, 'The Poetry of Karl Marx'

It is a happy thing that there is no royal road to poetry. The world should know by this time that one cannot reach Parnassus except by flying thither.

Yet from time to time more men go up and either perish in its gullies fluttering excelsior flags or else come down again with full folios and blank countenances. Yet the old fallacy keeps its ground. Every age has its false alarms.

> Gerard Manley Hopkins, 'Early Diaries'
> *Notebooks and Papers*

> Anyone can run to excesses,
> It is easy to shoot past the mark,
> It is hard to stand firm in the middle.
> Ezra Pound, XIII, *A Draft of Thirty Cantos*

It may happen that poets will be made more often by their sins than by their virtues, for general praise is unlucky, as the villages know, and not merely as I imagine—for I am superstitious about these things —because the praise of all but an equal enslaves and adds a pound to the ball at the ankle with every compliment.

> William Butler Yeats, 'Discoveries'
> *The Cutting of an Agate*

And here is the natural place to confess that any poet, dramatist, or novelist, who declares that he is indifferent whether or not people give him attention, is either an ass or a liar; anyhow, he is not natural.

> H. M. Tomlinson, 'The Problems of a Novelist'

What are the great poetical names of the last hundred years or so? Coleridge, Wordsworth, Byron, Shelley, Landor, Keats, Tennyson, Browning, Arnold, Morris, Rossetti, Swinburne—we may stop there. Of these, all but Keats, Browning, and Rossetti were University men; and of these three, Keats, who died young, cut off in his prime, was the only one not fairly well-to-do. It may seem a brutal thing to say, and it is a sad thing to say: but as a matter of hard fact the theory that poetical genius bloweth where it listeth, and equally in poor and rich, holds little truth. As a matter of hard fact, nine out of ten of these twelve were University men: which means that somehow or other they procured the means to get the best education England can give. As a matter of hard fact, you know that of the remaining three Browning was well-to-do, and I challenge you that, if he had not been well-to-do, he would no more have attained to writing *Saul*, or *The Ring and the Book*, than Ruskin would have attained to writing *Modern Painters* if his father had not dealt prosperously in business. Rossetti had a small private income; and moreover he painted. There remains but Keats; whom Atropos slew young, as she slew John Clare in a madhouse, and James Thomson by the laudanum he took to drug disappointment. These are dreadful facts, but let us face them. It is—however dishonouring to us as a nation—certain that by some fault in our commonwealth, the poor poet has not in these days, nor has he had for two hundred years, a dog's chance. Believe me—and I have spent a great part of the last ten years in watching some 320 Elementary Schools—we prate of democracy, but actually a poor child in England has little more hope than had the son of an Athenian slave to be emancipated into that intellectual freedom of which great writings are born.

A. Quiller-Couch, 'The Practice of Writing'
The Art of Writing

It does not speak favourably for the taste and humour of Detroit that its intelligentsia sniffed dire propaganda in Rivera's witchery; that it suspected anti-religious parody in the scene of a child being vaccinated. Nothing is to be thought of this except that a society dominated by captains of industry and their women folk will crave either the softest or the most exotic art.

Frank Jewett Mather, Jr.,
'Rivera's American Murals'

The public really love in art that which is banal and long familiar, that to which they have grown accustomed.

Chekov, *Notebooks*

I scarcely need to tell you that all the pioneer poets—even such poets as Wordsworth and Keats—have been disagreed with during their lifetime. The name of Wordsworth could not be mentioned until he was past fifty and sixty without an outburst of a vulgar nature from the press. It is not the slightest use for reviewers to fly into a temper and say that it is only the mad artists who are roughly treated by the crowd. For it can be proved that such treatment, varied by heart-breaking neglect, has been meted out to every artist since the time of Shakespeare.

Edith Sitwell, 'Experiment in Poetry'
Tradition and Experiment

And in spite of the immense amount of poetry published and read today, the personality truly and naturally poetic seems to be becoming rarer and rarer. It may be true that the kind of dignity and distinction which have been characteristic of the poet in the past are becoming more and more impossible in our modern democratic society and during a period when the ascendancy of scientific ideas has made man conscious of his kinship with the other animals and of his subjection to biological and physical laws rather than of his relation to the gods. It was easy for the lyric poet, from Wyatt's age to Waller's, to express himself both directly and elegantly, because he was a courtier, or, in any case, a member of a comparatively small educated class, whose speech combined the candour and naturalness of conversation among equals with the grace of a courtly society. It was possible for him honestly to take up a residence in an intellectual world where poetic images stood for actualities because the scientific language and technique for dealing with these actualities had not yet come to permeate thought. But the modern poet who would follow this tradition, and who would yet deal with life in any large way, must create for himself a special personality, must maintain a state of mind, which shall shut out or remain indifferent to many aspects of the contemporary world.

Edmund Wilson, Axel's Castle

> Hypocrisy and suave intrigue,
>   Successful impudence and lying,
> Lawlessness with law in league,
>   Talent in the gutter dying—
>   Cant,
>   Rant,
>   And superstition
> Are the favourites of Tradition—

Old French song

The man or boy of genius is very generally hated or scorned by the average man or boy until the day come for him to charm them into unwilling homage. Until that day he has often to cry with Blake, 'Why was I not born with a different face?' for his abstracted ways and strange interests arouse that hatred of the uncommon which lies deep in the common heart. It is said that if you tie a piece of red cloth to a sea-gull's leg its fellow-gulls will peck it to death. Shelley, tormented by the gull-like animosity of his school-fellows, plunged a pen through the hand of a tormentor. Blake leant out from a scaffolding where he sat at work and flung a Westminster student from a cornice, whither he had climbed the better to tease him.

William Butler Yeats,
Introduction to Blake's Poems

Those who are able to produce poor poetry, and whose friends know it, who yet refrain from exercising their acknowledged powers, enjoy the unqualified approval of the nine Muses.

Ik Mitchell, *Memoirs of an Editor*

Happy is it, that the mass of mankind eat and drink, and sleep, and perform their several tasks, and do as they like without us—caring nothing for our scribblings, our carpings, and our quibbles: and moving on the same, in spite of our fine-spun distinctions, fantastic theories, and lines of demarcation, which are like chalk-figures to be danced out before morning.

William Hazlitt, 'On the Conversation of Authors'

A man of talents, who shrinks from a collision with his equals or superiors, will soon sink below himself. We improve by trying our strength with others, not by showing it off. A person who shuts himself up in a little circle of dependents and admirers for fear of losing ground in his own opinion by jostling with the world at large, may continue to be gaped at by fools, but will forfeit the respect of sober and sensible men.

William Hazlitt, 'Characteristics'

The occasional poet is circumscribed by the narrowness of his subject. Whatever can happen to man has happened so often, that little remains for fancy or intervention. We have all been born; we have most of us been married; and so many have died be-

fore us, that our deaths can supply but few materials
for a poet.

Samuel Johnson, 'John Dryden', *Lives of the Poets*

Rhymes and rhymers pass away, poems distilled
    from poems pass away,
The swarms of reflectors and the polite pass, and
    leave ashes,
Admirers, importers, obedient persons, make but the
    soil of literature.
America justifies herself, give it time, no disguise can
    deceive it or conceal from it, it is impassive enough,
Only toward the likes of itself will it advance to
    meet them,
If its poets appear it will in due time advance to meet
    them, there is no fear of a mistake,
The proof of a poet shall be sternly deferred till his
    country absorbs him as affectionately as he has
    absorbed it.

Walt Whitman, 'By Blue Ontario's Shore'
Leaves of Grass

There are as many arts as there are artists—the
number is not seven, but countless as the stars. We
group them in constellation for our convenience, not
theirs; seven units are more easily handled than a
trillion. The confusions in regard to them are countless, too; the actual number is far greater; but they
may also be gathered for our convenience into seven
groups,—'seven' has the perfume of a mystic tradition kept fragrant by the superstition of generations

of men. So I begin with a roll-call of them: Poets write for money; poets are influenced by their environment; poets write in metres; poets write tragedies and comedies; poets are moral or immoral; poets are democratic or aristocratic; poets use figures of speech.
                J. E. Spingarn,
'The Seven Arts and the Seven Confusions'
Creative Criticism

A poet is no rattle-brain, saying what comes uppermost, and, because he says everything, saying, at last, something good; but a heart in unison with his time and country. The Genius of our life is jealous of individuals, and will not have any individual great, except through the general. There is no choice to genius. A great man does not wake up on some fine morning and say, 'I am full of life, I will go to sea, and find an Antarctic continent: today I will square the circle: I will ransack botany, and find a new food for man: I have a new architecture in my mind: I foresee a new mechanic power': no, but he finds himself in the river of thoughts and events, forced onward by the ideas and necessities of his contemporaries. He stands where all the eyes of men look one way, and their hands all point in the direction in which he should go.
          R. W. Emerson, 'Shakespeare'
Representative Men

And, talking of imagination, do you know the Black Thought, Gentlemen? I am loath to remind you of it in this fenced and pleasant place, but it is the one emotion that all men of imagination have in common. It is a horror of great darkness that drops upon a man unbidden, and drives him to think lucidly, connectedly, and with Cruikshank detail, of all the accidents whereby, through no fault of his own, he may be cut off from his work, and forced to leave those he loves defenceless to the world. You know the Black Thought, Gentlemen? It possesses some men in the dead of night; some in the sunshine; some when they are setting their palettes; some when they are stropping their razors; but only the very young, the very sound, the very single, are exempt.

Rudyard Kipling, *A Book of Words*

THE POET'S WORLD

WHEREVER a man opens his eyes on the world as a
poet, he is stricken into expression of its wonder,
its abundance and beauty, its lawful variety, or its
vigorous astonishments. This feeling makes the poet.
It may be cruelty or waste that astonishes him, but
he knows these things for their equalizing weight
in the scales of life. Or it may be patterns in the snowflake or the whirlwind he sees; or the recurrence of
human hope alternating with human chaos; a river
of time bringing wreckage past his look-out, then
ships steering under their own power. But it is always
as if he comes to his native land a stranger. Everything cries for his attention, and he sees what is perfect of its kind—perfectly good or perfectly bad.
Because he has never seen it before, it has never
been seen.

Chaucer had that fresh pleasure in life, and we may
believe he spoke for himself when he made the Wife
of Bath say, 'It tikleth me unto my herte rote that I
have had my world as in my tyme.' Shakespeare had
it; Hamlet was one of many who said for him, 'This
brave o'erhanging firmament'. George Herbert felt
it when he wrote

> The starres have us to bed,
> Night draws the curtain, which the sunne withdraws;
> Musick and light attend our head,
> All things unto our flesh are kinde
> In their descent and being; to our minde
> In their ascent and cause.

Keats, Donne, Pepys (he had the poet's eagerness) and Browning, and Hopkins, all relished life and the world, in its wholeness and in its infinite parts, writing with a capacity for excitement beyond that of most men.

When the poet tries to set down his vivid sense of his world, he may either chant the catalogue of its glories, or cry out its pains, or soar in a brief lyric concentration of the one loveliest moment of time. If he chants, then he piles up, like Chaucer, or Whitman, or Brooke, the bounty he has inherited. At the highest pitch is the 'Song to David' by Christopher Smart. If he turns his wonder to pure song, he cries like Gerard Manley Hopkins, 'Look, look up at the skies!' or like Emily Dickinson he catches up the little things of earth in a breathless run of words with a fierce light on them. Robinson Jeffers, standing a long way off from mankind, in his compassion says, 'You making haste haste on decay: not blameworthy; life is good, be it stubbornly long or suddenly a mortal splendor: meteors are not needed less than mountains: shine, perishing republic.' And the spirit of exaltation always smoulders, always ready to break into fire. When a well-meaning friend asked Blake, 'When the sun rises, do you not see a round disk of fire something like a guinea?' he said, 'Oh no, I see an immeasurable company of the heavenly host crying Holy Holy Holy is the Lord God Almighty.'

The poet sees in all things the extra dimension of time. Whatever his eye falls on is passing by, and he

knows it; he snatches at it with words, never recon-
ciled to its passing, yet delighting in its onward
show. English poetry is full of this haste, of Housman's 'Take my hand quick and tell me.' It has been
so ever since the unknown Anglo-Saxon wrote of
life, the bird, flying from the night and storm into
the bright banquet-hall, where song and fire glow,
and flying out again into the night. But the poet feels
the excitement more than the sadness of such a swift
passing. He stares, he touches, he runs to meet, and
in imagination throws himself into other lives, and
can never get enough. There crowds into his mind
an awareness of all that goes on in any moment of
time, with him or away from him, so that in poetry
he takes a long look forward and back into time and
across the world.

There also brims in him the love of things for their
own sake: the taste of food, the feeling of air on the
skin, the sound of voices, the look of trees in their
straightness, and the changes of light and weather
on roads, houses, hills, and the faces of men and
women. The weight of tools and weapons, the crash
of surf, man's brave architecture lifting roofs under
heaven, the smell of rain, and the ring of bells—he
loves these, and a thousand other reasons for not
dying.

But the poet is not always in the mood to see or
exult over light and abundance. Whatever it is that
poets are made of, it is partly salt. Living is sometimes despair and loss, and the black hour comes
when one cannot rejoice. At another hour correc-

tive satire breaks from poets harried and angered by
the difference between man's behaviour and man's
ideals. They strike to protect the life they cherish.
Yet the anger comes from the same man, and the same
source in the man, which is his intensity of consciousness. Either way the poet sees his world, his
work is to write down what he sees, and it is this
way, says Vernon Lee, 'being the response to man's
organized and unceasing cravings for strength, clearness, order, dignity and sweetness, for a life intenser
and more harmonious, that what man writes comes to
be greater than what man is.'

But there is always at bottom that earthy pleasure
in anything good of its kind; it makes any experience
vivid. His range seems to be several octaves more in
either direction than the ordinary instrument, and,
like a concert piano, he is tuned a half-note higher
for brilliant performance. He may have a vision as
vast as Milton's of lost paradise, or he may see with
Blake the world in a grain of sand. He may, like
Ralph Hodgson, 'hear the whole harmonious hymn
of being roll', or like Chaucer he may simply be
enormously amused by the perfection of charlatan-
ism in the wily Pardoner—the perfect rascal. The
poet needs only these representative bits of life to
make him remember all they stand for. At once he
sees the clean thrust of the blow struck, and feels
the pain of the one who falls under the blow. He
gets the satisfaction the striker gets, physically, and at
the same time he rouses to indignation for the defeated, beaten without cause and hopeless of striking

back. The poet may not take sides, one or the other;
the poet takes both sides, all sides. That is the work
he knows he has to do.

When in the world one side or the other would
conscript the poet in its service, arguing that it is his
duty, saying

> And now we hear
> All day in the dark stairway of the blood
> Rebellion climbing to that little room,
> The heart, there to demand great reckoning.
> We wait. We welcome one event so taut
> That action beats upon it like a drum,

then the poet, whose work it is to watch the world's
oppositions, and victories, and surrenders, will reply,

> Poetry runs to help that sharp tattoo,
> But all for its relish in the ultimate,
> To stretch itself in storm; as poetry would
> To be there first where time with streaming flags
> Declares new boundaries; as poetry would
> To marvel at a green tree wound with sun,
> To see a young man live almost unscarred,
> Mature in danger, passionate for peace,
> Who wears flesh tight about his bones and bright,
> His breath too quick for strangling, and his will,
> With caring for his generation, harsh.
> Poetry serves the living; rounds one hope
> Or all; gives grace, and sweeps that grace with light;
> Reminds all men that Time with sliding step,
> And Death with sudden stride, walk at their heels.
> But gives, warns, glorifies, in freedom best.
> Poetry flashes, cries, contends, rides hard.
> Poetry rings right, marvels, summons to life
> The soldier thoughts in arms lain down to sleep.
> But these: the bonfire burning in the rain,
> The moment made of light, the harvesters,
> The longed-for dead; all these are poetry.

And these: blind skull, blue wind, persistent love,
And change, and memory, and grief: all these.
The world is one to poetry: the hawk
That hovers marking down its prey, plunges,
And strikes, is ignorant of county names.

Someone has said that the sixth sense is an awareness of the gods, and the seventh a skill in nonsense.
An eighth may be memory. To a highly sensitive set
of the more usual five the poet adds these, and some
others. One of the others is a sense for words. Another is the sense of significance, which is the sense
that makes representative bits of life enough to
work with. The poet works also with the sense of
space, an airman's sight of the particular piece of
cosmos or geography where the poet stands. The
sight may be double and simultaneous. The sense of
time, the sense of structure, the sense of truth, also
reveal the world to the poet, and bring the world
straighter into his poem. But the sense of delight, or
wonder, or strangeness, whatever it may be named,
somehow quickens all these. It is not necessarily
pleasure, but it is always aliveness. The sense of wonder is the eye, so to speak, that lets life in to the mind,
the heart, the bone. The sense of wonder emphasizes
with Blake's 'bounding line and its infinite inflections
and movements' all his sensual and intellectual experience. The sense of wonder is the beginning of
poetry.

It is first necessary to see the world through the
poet's eyes, and get some understanding of this sense,
if we are to know what makes his work definite and

different. The secret lies in a special consciousness
of existence. The poet knows that he is. The poet
knows who he is. The poet knows where he is. He is
alive in time and space, the newest member of earth's
miraculous voyage. He is acutely aware of the
precarious exact crossing of his native latitude and
longitude, and of where to lay his hand upon the
subtle knot that makes him man. He stands there
open to the four seasons and the twelve winds; his
eyes are wide, his ears are keen, he feels earth hard
under the heel, and the blood rich in his body, and
he writes his poetry.

'MY HEART IN HIDING STIRRED'

It is now five of the clock, and the sun is going
apace on his journey: and fie sluggards, who would
be asleep: the bells ring to prayer, and the streets are
full of people, and the highways stored with travel-
ers: the scholars are up and going to school, and the
rods ready for the truants' correction: the maids are
at milking, and the servants at plough, and the wheel
goes merrily while the mistress is by: the capons
and the chickens must be served without door, and
the hogs cry till they have their swill: the shepard
is almost gotten to his fold, and the herd begins to
blow his horn through the town. The blind fiddler
is up with his dance and song, and the alehouse door
is unlocked for good fellows: the hounds begin to
cry after the hare, and horse and foot follow after

the cry: the traveller is now well on his way, and if
the weather be fair, he walks with the better cheer:
the carter merrily whistles to his horse, and the boy
with his sling casts stones at the crows: the lawyer
now begins to look at his case, and if he give good
counsel, he is worthy of his fee. . . .

Nicholas Breton, *The Fantasticks*

Strange the world about me lies,
Never yet familiar grown;
Still disturbs me with surprise,
Haunts me with a face half-known.

William Watson, 'World-Strangeness'

The world of girls' beautiful faces, bodies, and
clothes, quiet afternoons, graceful birds, great words,
tearful music, mind-joying poetry, beautiful livings,
loved things, known things: a to-be-used and known
and pleasure-to-be-giving world.

Eli Siegel, 'Hot Afternoons Have Been In Montana'
Prize Poems 1913-1929

The world is a dream, O Finn. The world is a
dream of our hearts. We can make it and mould it,
O captain, according to the shape of our will. With
truth, with courage and love, hard it would be not
to triumph. And if we are broken at last, the world
is a dream, O Finn.

Where we loved we are one. We are only what
we have remembered. The wave of Rughraidhe lash-

ing the shore, the lowing of oxen in Maghmaoin, the seagull's scream in distant Iorrus. The murmur of the streams in Sliabh Mis, the yell of the hounds at Drumlis, the noise of the fawns round Sliabh gCua. The hound's deep bay at twilight's fall and the barque's sharp grating on the shore. For where we have loved we are one.

Darrell Figgis, The Return of the Hero

One star fell, and another, as we walked.
Lifting his hand toward the west, he said—
How prodigal that sky is of its stars.
They fall and fall, and still the sky is sky.
Two more have gone, but heaven is heaven still.

Let us be reckless of our words and worlds,
And spend them freely as the tree his leaves;
And give them where the giving is most blest.
What should we save them for—a night of frost?
All lost for nothing, and ourselves a ghost.

Conrad Aiken, LVII, Preludes for Memnon

The spell of arms and voices: the white arms of roads, their promise of close embraces, and the black arms of ships that stand against the moon, their tale of distant nations. They are held out to say: we are alone—come.

James Joyce, *Portrait of the Artist as a Young Man*

It was but some days ago
When for my love and me, earth as of old
Made a green bed and drenched the air with gold,

And to our leaping pulse opposed her slow
Antiphony.
    Shaemas O'Sheel, 'Landscape With Figures 1850'

You never enjoy the world aright, till the Sea itself
floweth in your veins, till you are clothed with the
heavens, and crowned with the stars: and perceive
yourself to be sole heir of the world, and more than
so, because men are in it who are every one sole
heirs as well as you.
        Thomas Traherne, 'Centuries of Meditation'

When all we are is cut and set
Two crystals in Death's bracelet;
When all we have lies curved together
On God's long wing, like feather and feather,
It's probable that we'll forget
Climate and cloud and earth and weather.

Before we are dissolved in Light,
Or moulded motionless, on Flight,
Let us minutely move together,
Piteously promising one another,
Ecstatic midge and passionate mite—
To worship earth and relish weather.
                    Winifred Welles,
            'Song Before Entering Paradise Forever'
                    Blossoming Antlers

Till your pririt filleth the whole world, and the
stars are your jewels; till you are as familiar with the
ways of God in all Ages as with your walk and table:

till you are intimately acquainted with that shady
nothing out of which the world was made: till you
love men so as to desire their happiness, with a thirst
equal to the zeal of your own: till you delight in
God for being so good to all: you never enjoy the
world. Till you more feel it than your private estate,
and are more present in the hemisphere, considering
the beauties and the glories there, than in your own
house: Till you remember how lately you were
made, and how wonderful it was when you came
into it: and more rejoice in the palace of your glory,
than if it had been made today morning.

Thomas Traherne, 'Centuries of Meditation'

I saw Eternity the other night
Like a great ring of pure and endless light,
    All calm it was and bright;
And round it, Time, in hours, days, years,
    Driven by the spheres,
Like a vast shadow moved, in which the world
    And all her train were hurled.

Henry Vaughan, 'The World'

From the beginning, it has been native to all poets
and prophets. It is a condition dependent upon one
thing alone—a mood of wonder, childlike in its
freshness. What is man's great privilege, his excep-
tional experience? Consciousness and again consciousness, and it is in a passionate imaginative consciousness our true rewards are to be won.

Llewelyn Powys, *Now That the Gods are Dead*

Rightly to perceive a thing, in all the fulness of its qualities, is really to create it. So, on perfect holidays, you recreate the world and sign on again as a pleased and enthusiastic member of the great airship's company.   C. E. Montague, *The Right Place*

                    I hold him happiest
Who, before going quickly whence he came,
Hath looked ungrieving on these majesties,
The world-wide sun, the stars, waters, and clouds
And fire. Live, Parmeno, a hundred years
Or a few weeks, these thou wilt always see,
And never, never, any greater thing.
                                        Menander

Shakespeare, too, does not look at a thing, but into it, through it; so that he constructively comprehends it, can take it asunder and put it together again; the thing melts, as it were, into light under his eye, and anew creates itself before him. That is to say, he is a Poet. For Goethe, as for Shakespeare, the world lies all translucent, all fusible we might call it, encircled with wonder; the Natural in reality the Supernatural, for to the seer's eyes both become one.
                        Thomas Carlyle, 'Goethe'

    Look thy last on all things lovely
    Every hour. Let no night
    Seal thy sense in deathly slumber
        Till to delight
    Thou have paid thy utmost blessing;

Since that all things thou wouldst praise
Beauty took from those who loved them
In other days.

Walter de la Mare, 'Farewell'
Motley and Other Poems

I am always struck by the centrality of the observer's position. He always stands fronting the
middle of the arch, and does not suspect at first that
a thousand hills behold the sunset sky from equally
favourable positions.

H. D. Thoreau, *Journals*

Lord! What a stir Stankes makes, with his being
crowded in the streets, and wearied walking in London, and would not be wooed to go to a play, nor to
Whitehall, or to see the Lions, though he were carried in a coach. I never could have thought there had
been on earth a man so little curious in the world as
he is.

Samuel Pepys, *Diary*

The coolness of sheets, the warmth of blankets,
the look of the little blue flames dancing on the top
of a fire of hard coal, the taste of bread, or milk, or
honey, or wine or of oil, of well-baked potatoes,
or earth-tasting turnips!—the taste of the airs, dry or
moist, that blow in through our opened windows,
the look of the night-sky, the sounds of twilight or
of dawn, the hoarse monotone of a distant pine-wood
or of pebble-fretted waves—all these things as one

feels them are materials, eternal and yet fleeting, of the art of being alive upon the earth.

John Cowper Powys, *The Meaning of Culture*

This day and May 11 (1871) the bluebells in the little wood between the College and the highroad and in one of the Hurst Green cloughs. In the little wood, opposite the light, they stood in blackish spreads or sheddings like the spots on a snake. The heads are then like thongs and solemn in grain and grape-colour. But in the clough, through the light, they came in falls of sky-colour washing the brows and slacks of the ground with vein-blue, thickening at the double, vertical themselves and the young grass and brake fern combed vertical, but the brake struck the upright of all this with light winged tran-somes. It was a lovely sight. The bluebells in your hand baffle you with their inscape, made to every sense: if you draw your fingers through them they are lodged and struggle with a shock of wet heads; the long stalks rub and click and flatten to a fan on one another like your fingers across themselves would when you passed the palms hard across one another, making a brittle rub and jostle like the noise of a hurdle strained by leaning against; then there is the faint honey smell and in the mouth the sweet gum when you bite them. But this is easy, it is the eye they baffle. They give one a fancy of panpipes and of some wind instrument with stops—a trombone perhaps. The overhung necks—for growing they are little more than a staff with a simple crook but in water, where they stiffen, they take stronger turns, in the head like sheephooks or, when more waved throughout, like the waves riding through a ship that is being smacked—what with these overhung necks and what with the crisped ruffled bells dropping mostly on one side and the gloss these have at their footstalks they have an air of the knights at chess.

Gerard Manley Hopkins, 'Journal'
Notebooks and Papers

I am living this 27th day of June, 1847—a dull cloudy day and no sun shining. The clink of the smith's hammer sounds feebly over the roofs, and the wind is sighing gently as if dreaming of cheerfuller days. The farmer is ploughing in yonder fields, craftsmen are busy in the shops, the trader stands up in the counter, and all works go steadily forward.

H. D. Thoreau, *Journals*

Aug. 27—A day when all things are ours and possible, when things to write about, characters to interpret, stand out as clear as the dark still spruces against the bluest of blue skies.

Ruth Blodgett, Unpublished Notebooks

Life falls away from people who neglect
To seek its marvels; early are destroyed
The wilful stupid and the wilful blind.

Helene Mullins, 'Now Learn, O Cynic'
Streams from the Source

It is candle light. The fishes leap, the meadows
sparkle with the coppery light of fire-flies. The evening star, multiplied by undulating water, is like
bright sparks of fire continually ascending.

H. D. Thoreau, *Journals*

From my western balcony-window, I watched the
    light
Deepen under solid leaves along the hill
And under ledges I had never seen
On the mountain-range and sharpen the sides of
    boats . . .
And so it had been under my ribs with music
And with wine, a lovely deepening of the light
A body carries on its own small hill:
I laughed aloud, joining bright earth with earth.

Witter Bynner, 'Dawn', *Indian Earth*

I caught this morning morning's minion, King-
    dom of daylight's dauphin, dapple-dawn-drawn
    Falcon, in his riding
    Of the rolling level underneath him steady air,
    and striding
High there, how he rung upon the rein of a wimp-
    ling wing
In his ecstasy! Then off, off forth on swing,
    As a skate's heel sweeps smooth on a bow-bend:
    the hurl and gliding
    Rebuffed the big wind. My heart in hiding
Stirred for a bird,—the achieve of, the mastery of
    the thing!

Gerard Manley Hopkins, 'The Windhover'
Poems

The true spirit of delight, the exaltation, the sense of being more than man, which is the touchstone of the highest excellence, is to be found in mathematics as surely as in poetry. Real life is to most men a long second-best, a perpetual compromise between the ideal and the possible; but the world of pure reason knows no compromise, no practical limitations, no barrier to creative activity.

Bertrand Russell, 'The Study of Mathematics'
Philosophical Essays

Sing now the birds: on every bough a bird sings;
Slowly at first, then fast and faster,
Till the walled garden thrills and shrills with music:
The cricket beneath the violet aster

Cries his joy to heaven as the first beam strikes him—
The foxgloves bend beneath a weight of bees;
Praise! Praise! Praise! the chorus rises;
Drowsily, happily, dumbly sway the trees.

Conrad Aiken, *The Pilgrimage of Festus*

Eternity was manifest in the Light of the Day, and something infinite behind everything appeared: which talked with my expectation, and moved my desire. The city seemed to stand in Eden, or to be built in Heaven. The streets were mine, the temple was mine, the people were mine, their clothes and gold and silver were mine, as much as their sparkling eyes, fair skins and ruddy faces. The skies were mine, and so were the sun and moon and stars, and all the world was mine; and I the only spectator and enjoyer of it.

Thomas Traherne, 'Centuries of Meditation'

I put my ear to one of the posts, and it seemed as if every pore of the wood was filled with music, laboured with the strain—as if every fibre was affected and being seasoned or timed, rearranged according to a new and more harmonious law. Every swell and change or inflection of tone pervaded and seemed to proceed from the wood, the divine tree or wood, perchance—to keep it from rotting—to fill its pores with music!

H. D. Thoreau, *Journals*

Within, by a wildfire cedar-lit,
my fine green villains clasp their violins.

there was no lack of brilliant light. Our music
rose. There was the winding of the forest-horn,
and troubles, all that troop with music, raught us.

Eric Schroeder, 'The Winter Palace'

The heavens opened for the sunset tonight. When I had thought the day folded and sealed, came a burst of heavenly bright petals. I sat behind the window, pricked with rain, and looked until that hard thing in my breast melted and broke into the smallest fountain, murmuring as aforetime, and I drank the sky and the whisper.

Katherine Mansfield, *Journals*

Look at the stars! Look, look up at the skies!
O look at all the fire-folk sitting in the air!
The bright boroughs, the circle-citadels there!
Down in dim woods the diamond delves! the
    elves'-eyes!
The grey lawns cold where gold, where quick-
    gold lies!
Wind-beat white beam; airy abeles set on a flare!
Flake-doves sent floating forth at a farmyard
    scare!

    Gerard Manley Hopkins, 'The Starlight Night'
                          Poems

In his loneliness and fixedness he yearneth toward
the journeying Moon, and the stars that still sojourn,
yet still move onward; and everywhere the blue sky
belongs to them, and is their appointed rest and their
native country and their own natural home, which
they enter unannounced, as lords that are certainly
expected, and yet there is a silent joy at their arrival.

    S. T. Coleridge, Prose argument to
           The Ancient Mariner

The hand, that up the dark and twisted stair,
   Carries the tulip's candle in its case,
The shoulder and the thigh, that, straining, bear
   Up to their shelf each gossamer urn and vase,
Are tense and knotted, lean and veined and spare.
   Not with deft swiftness nor with delicate grace,

But in slow agonies of strength and care,
  The burden of a flower's ephemeral face
Is lifted and unhooded in the air.
                Winifred Welles, 'The Body of the Roots'
                    Blossoming Antler

The Horned Violet is a pretty thing, gracefully
lashed. Even in withering the flower ran through
beautiful inscapes by the screwing up of the petals
into straight little barrels or tubes. It is not that inscape does not govern the behaviour of things in
slack and decay as one can see even in the pining of
the skin in the old and even in a skeleton but that
horror prepossesses the mind, but in this case there
was nothing in itself to shew even whether the flower
were shutting or opening.
                Gerard Manley Hopkins, Journal 1871,
                    Notebooks and Papers

To mount a hill is to lift with you something light-
er and brighter than yourself or than any meaner
burden. You lift the world, you raise the horizon;
you give a signal for the distance to stand up. It is
like the scene in the Vatican when a Cardinal, with
his dramatic Italian hands, bids the kneeling groups
arise. He does more than bid them. He lifts them,
he gathers them up, far and near, with the upward
gesture of his expressive force. Or it is as when a conductor takes his players to successive heights of
music. You summon the sea, you bring the moun-

tains, the distances unfold unlooked-for wings and take an even flight. You are but a man lifting his weight on the upward road, but as you climb the circle of the world goes up to face you.

Alice Meynell, *The Spirit of Place*

I got up the mountain edge, and from the top saw the world stretcht out—cornlands and forest, the river winding among meadow-flats, and right off, like a hem of the sky, the moving sea, with snatches of foam, and large ships reaching forward, out-bound. And then I thought no more, but my heart leapt to meet the wind, and I ran, and ran. I felt my legs under me, I felt the wind buffet me, hit me on the cheek; the sun shone, the bees swept past me singing; and I too sang, shouted, World, World, I am coming!

Maurice Hewlett, *Pan and the Young Shepherd*

This light is the very flush of spring; it is innocent
    and warm;
It is gentle as celestial rain; it is mellow as gold;
Its pure effulgence may unbind the form
Of a blossoming tree; it may quicken fallow mould.

This light is various and strange; its luminous hue
May transmute the bleakest dust to silver snow;
Its radiance may be caught within a pool, a bead of
    dew;
It may contract to the sheerest point; it may arch to
    a bow.

This light is heaven's transcendant boon, a beam
Of infinite calm; it will never cease;
It will illuminate forever the aether-stream;
This light alone can lead me to peace.

Theodore Roethke, 'This Light'

What is marvellous? what is impossible or vague?
after you have just once opened the space of a peach-
pit and given audience to the far and near and to the
sunset and had all things enter with electric swiftness softly and duly without confusion or jostling
or jam.

Walt Whitman, Preface to *Leaves of Grass*, 1855

First saw the Northern Lights. My eye was caught
by beams of light and dark very like the crown of
horny rays the sun makes behind a cloud. At first I
thought of silvery cloud until I saw that these were
more luminous and did not dim the clearness of the
stars in the Bear. They rose slightly radiating thrown
out from the earthline. Then I saw soft pulses of
light one after another rise and pass upwards arched
in shape but waveringly and with the arch broken.
They seemed to float, not following the warp of the
sphere as falling stars look to do but free though
concentrical with it. This busy working of nature
wholly independent of the earth and seeming to go
on in a strain of time not reckoned by our reckoning
of days and years but simpler and as if correcting the
preoccupation of the world by being preoccupied
with and appealing to and dated to the day of judge-

ment was like a new witness to God and filled me
with delightful fear.

> Gerard Manley Hopkins, Journal 1870,
> *Notebooks and Papers*

How silent, how spacious, with room for all, yet
without place to insert an atom,—in graceful succession, in equal fulness, in balanced beauty, the dance
of the hours goes forward still. Like an odour of
incense, like a strain of music, like a sleep, it is inexact and boundless. It will not be dissected, nor
unravelled, nor shown.

> R. W. Emerson, 'Nature', *Conduct of Life*

Nevertheless it is the eve. Let us accept all inflows
of vigour and real tenderness. And at dawn, armed
with an eager patience, we shall enter splendid
towns.

> Rimbaud, *Une Saison en Enfer*

The light in her beautiful, formal room was dim,
though it would do, as everything would always do;
the hot wind had kept out lamps, but there was a
pair of clusters of candles that glimmered over the
chimney-piece like the tall tapers of an altar. The
windows were all open, their redundant hangings
swaying a little, and he heard once more, from the
empty court, the small plash of the fountain. From
beyond this, and as from a great distance—beyond
the court, beyond the *corps de logis* forming the
front—came, as if excited and exciting, the vague
voice of Paris. Strether had all along been subject

to sudden gusts of fancy in connection with such matters as these—odd starts of the historical sense, suppositions and divinations with no warrant but their intensity. Thus and so, on the eve of great recorded dates, the days and nights of revolution, the sounds had come in, the omens, the beginnings broken out.

Henry James, *The Ambassadors*

We do not commonly live our life out to the full; we do not fill all our pores with our blood; we do not inspire and expire fully and entirely enough, so that the wave, the comber of each inspiration shall break upon our extremest shores, rolling till it meets the sea which bounds us, and the sound of the surf comes back to us. Might not a bellows assist us to breathe? That our breathing should create a wind on a calm day! We live but a fraction of our life. Why do we not let on the flood, raise the gates, and set all our wheels in motion? He that hath ears to hear, let him hear.

H. D. Thoreau, *Journals*

THE POET'S NATURE

ANY description of the poet as human being, or as poet, for that matter, must indicate his inclusiveness. Though his range is widely extensive and deeply intensive, he springs to attention at any border, at any level. He can be Hamlet, or Falstaff. He can be Macduff, as Whitman meant when he said that he, too, 'knitted the old knot of contrariety, had guile, lust, hot wishes I dared not speak, was wayward, vain, greedy, shallow.' But there is also John Keats, 'happy as a man can be . . . with the yearning passion I have for the beautiful, connected and made one with the ambition of my intellect', and there is William Butler Yeats, 'blest by everything, everything I look upon is blest', in one mood, or in another 'timid, entangled, empty and abashed'. Crosland thrusts forward his 'furious wise will and heart of stone', and D. H. Lawrence cries out his passionate conviction that 'My great religion is a belief in the blood!' Sir Thomas Browne had 'all Africa and her prodigies' in him. Conrad Aiken bids his readers with him 'laugh with fool's delight that heavenly folly made the world so bright.'

The poet, Bliss Perry once said, has always been 'genus irritable'—the irritable kind. But not, of course, in the ordinary sense. He is easily irritated— that is, easily stirred, awaked, roused into words; quickly made glad; often driven to excesses of im-

patience, anger, exaltation, love, terror. John Donne
must have the soul descend to affections, 'else a great
Prince in prison lies'; and Shakespeare marks 'the
expense of spirit in a waste of shame'; Masefield re-
members as most poets do that 'man with his burning
soul has but an hour of breath'; Emerson walks across
Cambridge Common, 'glad almost to the brink of
fear'; and Katherine Mansfield in the grimness of
grief writes in her journal, 'Today I am hardening
my heart. I am walking all around my heart and
building up the defences'; Keats feels 'an awful
warmth about my heart like a load of immortality'.
All these, poured out though they are extravagant-
ly on the page, are not a fraction of the poet's capacity
and variety. There was Milton, who knew the courts
of heaven, and Villon, who knew the alleys of Paris.
Chaucer rode down to Canterbury with priests, ship-
men, millers, knights, and nuns; George Herbert
lived in the retirement of a country parish and his
mother's house. Blake was mad. Or was he sane? And
Alexander Pope was very sane.

'Not only poems, but songs, snatches, and raptures
of a flaming spirit', said a seventeenth-century writer,
of the psalms of David. It is the heat of the blood
that differentiates the poet. It was clever of Oscar
Wilde to say that several drinks of whiskey can produce an effect very similar to intoxication. But in
one of the finest of short poems in English, James
Thomson says, 'He reeleth with his own heart, that
great rich vine.'

And it is not an accident that the poet is articulate; sometimes one feels that writers of all kinds have an unfair advantage of the rest of the world, because they can get a hearing for their pains and joys; as if no one else felt pain and joy at all. Sometimes this deludes the poet into the smugness of naming himself the voice of the silent; self-elected. But the special quality of the poet begins with the involuntary voice. With such a necessity laid on him, seeing as he does a golden outline that defines everything between himself and the sun, he may not silence the sense of vivid life in himself. It beats and surges into a declaration of being, an emphatic I Am: the world was thus when I was in it—active, growing, decaying, complex, passionate, pitiful, miraculous. It is simply that a current passes through his body; sometimes it convulses him with its enormous voltage, but more often he is a good conductor, pure metal, and passes on the flow of life to later times and other men. Poetry for this (figurative) reason is dangerous to read, like touching a bare wire, for people who are afraid of the life in the wires.

Because the drift of days seldom makes the average man shiver and glow with the sudden shock of the whole meaning of life, he feels in the unusual behaviour of the poet something deplorable, because it is unusual. The average man has also had unpleasant experience of the poet of mixed baser metal, the imperfect conductor of the current. But the real poet is a norm for mankind: in the quality of his living the man all would wish to be. T.W.H. Crosland reminds us of the old falsehood that a writer of

poems, especially of sonnets, is a person in precarious
health, or of abnormal behaviour. But, he says, as a
matter of fact, the great poets 'are not only the
sanest people in the world, but physically and temperamentally the toughest.' Men and women weak
in body and nerves burn out after a little of the current has passed through them; they cannot stand it.
But in the great spirits, such as Shakespeare, Goethe,
Dante, Chaucer, or Yeats, there is a calmness and a
confident strength. They are in accord with the force
flowing through them; there is room enough in
them, and there are no obstructions.

But metaphors are a view from one side. To speak
of poets as good conductors is to imply passive re-
ception and release; the figure is not the whole truth.
This is because the poet also imparts a special quality
to the life flowing through him, so that it is changed
by the passage. One element of this change is the
new rhythm that he gives to the stream of life. It has
been his study to discover his special inner rhythm;
all life that enters his perception beats thereafter to
that unmistakable vibration. He also colours the life
he feels with his powerful affection for it, which
is another sort of change. Proust, though not a versi-
fier, transmitted his sense of life coloured by caring
over the detail of every scene and hour, reluctant to
be called away even to the next hour and the following episode. It may be that a sharp sense of the apal-
ling limits of time is what makes the poets wish to
linger and intensify. But after all, the poet is one who,
because he feels in the air time rushing by, knows

more than most about it, and has power over it. He can stop time. By his passionately scrupulous examination of one moment, he can recreate it as it is and let it go, knowing as Wycliff knew that 'word, wynde, and mannes mind is full short, but letter written dwelleth.' The poet, who can free all men as well as himself from time, loves what he writes of, and writes of what he loves. If he protests, if he mourns, if he hates, and writes about that, his love is not far; it is that powerful affection thwarted of which he speaks. And to a certain extent he loves the hateful thing, if only it has life in it. 'As to the poetic character itself,' wrote Keats in a letter, 'it lives in gusto, be it foul or fair, high or low, rich or poor, mean or elevated—it has as much delight in conceiving an Iago as an Imogen.'

Wherever the poet stands, the hills and houses and the thinking of mankind centre on him like the spokes of a wheel or the threads of a spider's web. He looks out in every direction with as fresh an excitement as if the world had never been thrust upon the eyes of men till then. This is a mad conviction, but it is the key to the mystery, what Goethe calls 'the open secret,' open to all, seen by almost none. It never occurs to him not to dare say what he sees; to him it is an overwhelming wonder that he is there at all, and it seems only natural that so placed he should communicate his astonishment and delight. This confidence is an element of genius, but every poet shares it. He feels a kind of godhead; not egotistic assumption, but the fulness of life and his near-

ness to the source. In vision he has space and time for
latitude, as well as such intense apprehension that the
commonplace is miraculous and the near-at-hand a
wonder fetched home for his pleasure. Wherever
the scale of things seems meagre to him, because the
gods were tired, or daylight not illumination enough,
he heightens through his own creativeness the proportions, and he focuses a single beam of light which
the sun shall not dim by going down. When natural
music is faint to the ears of mankind, the poet magnifies it. Gaps in the created order are his to fill, or
at the least to foresee; and the future, however im-
penetrable a curtain it seems to drop between it and
ourselves, is his to prophesy. To do these things: to
sharpen, to re-enforce, to heighten, to prophesy, is
to exercise his highest power, that of creator.

'THE MAN AWARE OF HIMSELF'

Here was a task as great as the world. And he who
stood before it and beheld it was unknown and strug-
gling under the necessity of earning his bread. He
was quite alone, and if he had been a real dreamer,
he would have dreamed a deep and beautiful dream—
one of those long, long dreams in which a life would
pass like a day. But this young man who worked in
the factory at Sèvres was a dreamer whose dream
rose in his hands and he began immediately its reali-
zation. He sensed where he had to begin. A quietude
which was in him showed him the wise road. Here

already Rodin's deep harmony with nature revealed
itself; that harmony which the poet George Roden-
bach calls an elemental power. And, indeed, it is an
underlying patience in Rodin which renders him so
great; a silent, superior forbearance resembling the
wonderful patience and kindness of Nature that begins creation with a trifle in order to proceed silently
and steadily toward abundant consummation. Rodin
did not presume to create the tree in its full growth.
He began with the seed beneath the earth as it were.
And this seed grew downward, sunk deep its roots
and anchored them before it began to shoot upward
in the form of a young sprout. This required time,
time that lengthened into years. 'One must not
hurry,' said Rodin to the few friends who gathered
about him, in answer to their urgence.

Rainer Maria Rilke, *Auguste Rodin*

I am not a liberal, not a conservative, not a be-
liever in gradual progress, not a monk, not an in-
differentist. I should like to be a free artist and nothing more. I regard trade-marks and labels as a superstition. My holy of holies is the human body, health,
intelligence, talent, inspiration, love, and the most
absolute freedom—freedom from violence and lying, whatever forms they may take. This is the pro-
gramme I would follow if I were an artist.

Chekov, *Letters*

Now it appears to me that almost any man may
like the spider spin from his own inwards his own

airy citadel—the points of leaves and twigs on which
the spider begins her work are few, and she fills the
air with a beautiful circuiting.

John Keats, *Letters*

> The feast of love is music,
> And the wine of love is song.
> When love sits down to the banquet,
> Love sits long,
>
> Sits long, and arises drunken,
> But not with the feast and the wine.
> He reeleth with his own heart,
> That great, rich Vine.

James Thomson, 'The Vine'

The great angels of annunciation create the beauty
of their own real names. Who now finds Shakespeare
ridiculous? And how lovely a name is Keats?

Havelock Ellis, 'The Art of Writing'
The Dance of Life

The Genius of Poetry must work out its own sal-
vation in a man: It can not be matured by law and
precept, but by sensation and watchfulness in itself
—That which is creative and must create itself—In
Endymion, I leaped headlong into the sea, and thereby have become better acquainted with the Sound-
ings, the quicksands, and the rocks, than if I had
stayed upon the green shore, and piped a silly pipe,
and took tea and comfortable advice. I was never

afraid of failure; for I would sooner fail than not be
among the greatest.   John Keats, *Letters*

> Often we must entertain,
> Tolerantly if we can,
> Ancestors returned again
> Trying to be modern man.
> Gates of memory are wide;
> All of them can shuffle in,
> Join the family, and, once inside,
> Alas, what a disturbance they begin!
> Creatures of another time and mood,
> They wrangle, they dictate;
> Bawl their experience into brain and blood,
> Call themselves Fate.
>
>   Harold Monro, *Strange Meetings*

A man of adequate vitality and zest will surmount
all misfortunes by the emergence after each blow
of an interest in life and the world which cannot be
narrowed down so much as to make one loss fatal.
To be defeated by one loss or even by several is not
something to be admired as a proof of sensibility,
but something to be deplored as a failure in vitality.
All our affections are at the mercy of death, which
may strike down those whom we love at any moment. It is therefore necessary that our lives should
not have that narrow intensity which puts the whole
meaning and purpose of our life at the mercy of an
accident.

Bertrand Russell, *The Conquest of Happiness*

Joy is man's passage from a lesser to a greater perfection.

Spinoza, 'The Origin and Nature of the Emotions'
Ethics

Look thou within: within thee is the fountain of good, and it will ever spring, if thou wilt ever delve.

Marcus Aurelius

My great religion is a belief in the blood, the flesh, as being wiser than the intellect. We can go wrong in our minds. But what our blood feels and believes and says, is always true. The intellect is only a bit and a bridle. What do I care about knowledge? All I want is the answer to my blood, direct, without fribbling intervention of mind, or moral, or whatnot. I conceive a man's body as a kind of flame, like a candle-flame, forever upright and yet flowing: and the intellect is just the light that is shed on to the things around. And I am not so much concerned with the things around—which is really mind—but with the mystery of the flame forever flowing, coming God knows how from out of practically nowhere, and being itself, whatever there is around it, that lights it up. We have got so ridiculously mindful, that we never know that we ourselves are anything—we think there are only the objects we shine upon. And there the poor flame goes on burning ignored, to produce this light. And instead of chasing the mystery in the fugitive, half-lighted things

outside us, we ought to look at ourselves, and say,
'My God, I am Myself!'

D. H. Lawrence, Letters

Come, said my soul,
Such verses for my body let us write, (for we are
    one)
That should I after death invisibly return,
Or, long, long hence, in other spheres,
There to some group of mates the chants resuming,
(Tallying earth's soil, trees, winds, tumultuous
    waves,)
Ever with pleased smile I may keep on,
Ever and ever yet the verses owning—as, first, I here
    and now,
Signing for soul and body, set to them my name.

Walt Whitman, Invocation to Leaves of Grass

I believe I can tell the particular little chances that
filled my head first with such chimes of verse, as have
never since left ringing there; for I remember, when
I began to read, and to take some pleasure in it, there
was wont to lie in my mother's parlor (I know not
by what accident, for she herself never in her life
read any book but of devotion) but there was wont
to lie Spenser's works. This I happened to fall upon,
and was infinitely delighted with the stories of the
knights, and giants, and monsters, and brave houses,
which I found everywhere there (though my understanding had little to do with all this) and by degrees, with the tinkling of the rhyme and dance of

the numbers; so that, I think, I had read him all over before I was twelve years old, and was thus made a poet. Abraham Cowley, 'Of Myself'

Ah! but verses amount to so little when one begins to write them young. One ought to wait and gather sense and sweetness a whole life long, and a long life is possible, and then, quite at the end, one might perhaps be able to write ten good lines. For verses are not, as people imagine, simple feelings (we have these soon enough); they are experiences. In order to write a single verse, one must see many cities, and men and things; one must know animals and the flight of birds, and the gestures that the little flowers make when they open out in the morning. One must be able to return in thought to roads in unknown regions, to unexpected encounters, and to partings that had been long foreseen; to days of childhood that are still indistinct, and to parents whom one had to hurt when they sought to give some pleasure which one did not understand (it would have been a pleasure to someone else); to childhood's illnesses that so strangely begin with such a number of profound and grave transformations, to days spent in rooms withdrawn and quiet, and to mornings by the sea, to the sea itself, to oceans, to nights of travel that rushed along loftily and flew with all the stars—and still it is not enough to be able to think of all this. There must be memories of many nights of love, each one unlike the others, of the screams of women in labour, and of women in childbed, light and blanched and sleeping, shutting themselves in. But one must also have been beside the dying, must have sat beside the dead in a room with open windows and with fitful noises. One must be able to forget them when they are many and one must have the immense patience to wait until they come again. For it is the memories themselves that matter. Only when they have turned to blood within us, to glance and gestured, nameless and no longer to be distinguished from ourselves—only then can it happen that in a most rare hour the first word of a poem arises in their midst and goes forth from them.

Rainer Maria Rilke,
The Notebook of Malta Laurids Brigge

The man who is aware of himself is henceforward independent; and he is never bored, and life is only too short, and he is steeped through and through with a profound yet temperate happiness. He alone lives, while other people, slaves of ceremony, let life slip past them in a kind of dream. Once conform, once do what other people do because they do it, and a lethargy steals over all the finer nerves and faculties of the soul. She becomes all outer show and inward emptiness; dull, callous, and indifferent.

Virginia Woolf, 'Montaigne'
The Common Reader

I have written this that you might see I have my share of the highest pleasure, and that though I may choose to pass my days alone, I shall be no solitary.

The only thing that can ever affect me personally
for more than one short passing day is any doubt
about my powers for poetry: I seldom have any,
and I look with hope to the nighing time when I
shall have none. I am as happy as a man can be, with
a yearning passion I have for the beautiful, connected and made one with the ambition of my intellect.   John Keats, *Letters*

> The poet mused upon the dusky height,
>   Between two stars towards night,
> His purpose in his heart. I watched, a space,
>   The meaning of his face:
> There was the secret, fled from earth and skies,
>   Hid in his grey young eyes.
> My heart and all the Summer wait his choice,
>   And wonder for his voice.
> Who shall foretell his songs, and who aspire
>   But to divine his lyre?
> Sweet earth, we know thy dimmest mysteries,
>   But he is lord of his.
>   Alice Meynell, 'In Early Spring', *Poems*

'Why are thy songs so short?' a bird was once
asked. 'Is it because thou art short of breath?'
   'I have very many songs, and I should like to sing
them all.'   Daudet, copied in Chekov's *Notebook*

I do not ask of God that He should change anything in events, but that He should change me in
regard to things, so that I might have the power to

create my own universe about me, to govern my
dreams, instead of enduring them.

> Gérard de Nerval

.

It is essential in this world to be indifferent. Only
those who are indifferent are able to see things clearly, to be just, and to work. Of course, I am only
speaking of intelligent people of fine natures; the
empty and selfish are indifferent anyway.

> Chekov, *Letters*

> Ah, when to the heart of man
>   Was it ever less than a treason
> To go with the drift of things,
>   To yield with a grace to reason,
> And bow and accept the end
>   Of a love or a season?

> Robert Frost, 'Reluctance', *A Boy's Will*

It is said that a poet has died young in the breast
of the most stolid. It may be contended, rather, that
this (somewhat minor) bard in almost every case
survives, and is the spice of life to his possessor. Jus-
tice is not done to the versatility and unplumbed
childishness of man's imagination. His life from
without may seem but a rude mound of mud; there
will be some golden chamber at the heart of it, in
which he dwells delighted; and for as dark as his
pathway seems to the observer, he will have some
kind of bull's eye at his belt.

> R. L. Stevenson, 'The Lantern-Bearers'
> *Across the Plains*

Rave how thou wilt; unmoved, remote,
That inward presence slumbers not,
Frets out each secret from thy breast,
Gives thee no rally, pause, or rest,
Scans close thy very thoughts, lest they
Should sap his patient power away,
Answers thy wrath with peace, thy cry
With tenderest taciturnity.

   Walter de la Mare, 'Haunted', *The Listeners*

I felt my own smile with my fingers—and lost it at once. No matter; it was certainly I who had inspired this concerted impulse of the fingers; something more than the bone was demonstrably mine, then—something called inspiration. Their impulse had depended on my inspiration, expressed by my bones, plus a reflecting machine called a mirror. I was therefore free among all these prisoners; I could disentangle myself from this snare of mirrors—they, never. I was the original, they the substitutes; I was the music, they the gramophone records.

   Stella Benson, 'Reflections in a Mirror'

When such as I cast out remorse
So great a sweetness flows into the breast
We must laugh and we must sing,
We are blest by everything,
Everything we look upon is blest.

        William Butler Yeats
        'Dialogue of Self and Soul'
        The Winding Stair

The poets who describe Nature most minutely
and most faithfully are not usually the great poets.
That is intelligible because the poet—even the poet
in the wide sense who also uses prose—is primarily
the instrument of human emotion and not of scientific observation. Yet that poet possesses immense re-
sources of strength who early in life has stored within him the minute knowledge of some field of the
actual external world.

> Havelock Ellis, 'The Art of Writing'
> *The Dance of Life*

Emphatically may it be said of the poet, as Shakespeare hath said of man, that 'he looks before and after'. He is the rock of defence for human nature;
an upholder and preserver, carrying everywhere
with him relationship and love. In spite of differences
of soil and climate, of language and manners, of laws
and customs: in spite of things silently gone out of
mind, and things violently destroyed; the poet binds
together by passion and knowledge the vast empire
of human society, as it is spread over the whole
earth, and over all time.

> W. Wordsworth, Preface to *Lyrical Ballads*

Earth's wheels run oiled with blood. Forget we that.
Let us lie down and dig ourselves in thought.
Beauty is yours and you have mastery.
Wisdom is mine and I have mystery.
We two will stay behind and keep our troth.
Let us forego men's minds that are brutes' natures,

Let us not sup the blood which some say nurtures,
Be we not swift with swiftness of the tigress.
Let us break ranks from those who trek from pro-
    gress.
Miss we the march of this retreating world
Into old citadels that are not walled.
Let us lie out and hold the open truth.

> Wilfred Owen, An early version of
> 'Strange Meetings', *Poems*

But poets, or those who imagine and express this indestructible order, are not only the authors of language and of music, of the dance and architecture and painting: they are the institutors of laws, and the founders of civil society and the inventors of the arts of life, and the teachers, who draw into a certain propinquity with the beautiful and the true that partial apprehension of the agencies of the invisible world which is called religion. Hence all original relations are allegorical, or susceptible of allegory, and like Janus have a double face of false and true. Poets, according to the circumstances of the age and nation in which they appeared were called in the earlier epochs of the world legislators or prophets: a poet essentially comprises and unites both these characters. For he not only beholds intensely the present as it is, but he beholds the future in the present, and his thoughts are the germs of the flower and the fruit of the latest time.

> P. B. Shelley, *Defence of Poetry*

No live man is without an arbitrary passion for some experience. Indeed, the defect of many of those most scornful of poetry is not that they are strong in the practical life, but that the attachment to some single state has got the better of them. The greatly poetic differ from them only in the healthy variety of their loves, prevailing everywhere and always.   Max Eastman, 'Poetic People'
                    The Enjoyment of Poetry

Love at the lips was touch
As sweet as I could bear;
And once that seemed too much;
I lived on air

That crossed me from sweet things,
The flow of—was it musk
From hidden grapevine springs
Down hill at dusk?

I had the swirl and ache
From sprays of honeysuckle
That when they're gathered shake
Dew on the knuckle.

I craved strong sweets, but those
Seemed strong when I was young;
The petal of the rose
It was that stung.

Now no joy but lacks salt
That is not dashed with pain

And weariness and fault;
I crave the stain

Of tears, the aftermark
Of almost too much love,
The sweet of bitter bark
And burning clove.

When stiff and sore and scarred
I take away my hand
From leaning on it hard
In grass and sand,

The hurt is not enough:
I long for weight and strength
To feel the earth as rough
To all my length.

    Robert Frost, 'To Earthward' *New Hampshire*

It is not in his personal emotions, the emotions pro-
voked by particular events in his life, that the poet
is in any way remarkable or interesting. His particular emotions may be simple, or crude, or flat. The
emotion in his poetry will be a very complex thing,
but not with the complexity of the emotions of people who have very complex or unusual emotions in
life. One error, in fact, of eccentricity in poetry is
to seek for new human emotions to express; and in
this search for novelty in the wrong place it dis-
covers the perverse. The business of the poet is not to
find new emotions but to use the ordinary ones and,
in working them up into poetry, to express feelings

which are not in actual emotions at all. And emotions which he has never experienced will serve his turn as well as those familiar to him. Consequently, we must believe that 'emotion recollected in tranquillity' is an inexact formula. For it is neither emotion, nor recollection, nor, without distortion of meaning, tranquillity. It is a concentration, and a new thing resulting from the concentration, of a very great number of experiences which to the practical and active person would not seem to be experiences at all; it is a concentration which does not happen consciously or of deliberation. These experiences are not 'recollected' and they finally unite in an atmosphere which is 'tranquil' only in that it is a passive attending upon the event. Of course this is not quite the whole story. There is a great deal, in the writing of poetry, which must be conscious and deliberate. In fact, the bad poet is usually unconscious where he ought to be conscious, and conscious where he ought to be unconscious.

T. S. Eliot, 'Tradition and the Individual Talent'
Selected Essays 1917-1932

The mass of men are very unpoetic, yet that Adam that names things is always a poet.

H. D. Thoreau, *Journals*

So long as a man likes the splashing of a fish, he is a poet; but when he knows that the splashing is nothing but the chase of the weak by the strong, he is a thinker; but when he does not understand what

sense there is in the chase, or what use the equili-
brium which results from destruction, he is becoming
silly and dull, as he was when he was a child.

Chekov, *Notebooks*

Poets—the best of them, are a very chameleonic
race; they take the colour not only of what they feed
on, but of the very leaves under which they pass.

P. B. Shelley, *Letters*

As to the poetic character itself (I mean that sort,
of which, if I am anything, I am a member; that sort
distinguished from the Wordsworthian, or egotis-
tical sublime), it is not itself—it has no self—it is
everything and nothing—it has no character—it enjoys light and shade—it lives in gusto, be it foul or
fair, high or low, rich or poor, mean or elevated—
it has as much delight in conceiving an Iago as an
Imogen. A poet is the most unpoetical of anything
in existence, because he has no identity; he is constantly in for, and filling, some other body.

John Keats, *Letters*

What is the poet's ecstasy? A flying.
The soul, unjessed, darts upward, crying, crying,
The spirit flowing and the body drying.

There in a country where no self can blind it,
The soul goes flying with no past behind it
And neither friend nor enemy can find it.

Eileen Duggan, 'Ecstasy', *Poems*

David's Psalms are not only poems but songs, snatches and raptures of a flaming spirit. And this indeed I observe to the honour of poets; I never found them covetous or scrapingly base. The Jews had not two such kings in all their catalogue, as Salomon and his father, poets both. There is a largeness in their souls beyond the narrowness of other men; and why may we not then think, this may embrace more both of heaven and of God? I cannot but conjecture this to be the reason that they, most of them, are poor; they find their minds so solaced with their own flights that they neglect the study of growing rich. Besides, they are for the most part mighty lovers of their palates, and this is a known impoverisher. And they are all friends to the grape and liquor, though I think many, more out of a ductile nature and their love to pleasant company, than their affection to the juice alone. They are all of free natures, and are the truest definition of that philosopher's man, which gives him animal risible. Their grossest fault is that you may conclude them sensual, yet this does not touch them at all. Ingenious for the most part they are. I know there be some rhyming fools; but what have they to do with poetry?

Owen Feltham, 'Of Poets and Poetry'

Poet and Prophet differ greatly in our loose modern notions of them. In some old languages, again, the titles are synonymous; Vates means both Prophet and Poet: and indeed at all times, Prophet and Poet, well understood, have much kindred of

meaning. Fundamentally indeed they are still the same; in this most important respect especially, that they have penetrated both of them into the sacred mystery of the Universe; what Goethe calls 'the open secret.' 'Which is the great secret?' asks one.— 'The open secret,'—open to all, seen by almost none.
Thomas Carlyle, 'The Hero as Poet'
On Heroes, Hero-Worship, and the
Heroic in History

Among primitive men the poet is merely one of many whom a group experience has wrought up emotionally to such a pitch that a liberation from excitement is as strongly desired as the satisfaction of a physical need. From the group of the mourners, the rejoicing, the enraged, the terror-stricken, there leaps forth one in whom the passion common to all has crystallized into intelligible speech; another leaps forth, perhaps a third. And each time the group of bystanders expresses its assent and inner liberation by cries and ululations. Here we observe that the poet has no existence separate from the tribe. The excitement once passed, he is a mere tribal unit like any other. He makes no demand of his tribe; the tribe makes no demand of him.

Nevertheless we shall have to assume even in this 'precentor' of primitive times a specific gift: in some small measure, at least, a god gave him, above his brethren, the power to utter what he suffered. If and whenever this individual gift was heightened, the man in question became capable of reacting to stimuli not powerful enough to excite the tribal group. He no longer uttered his cry only under the immediate stimulus of death, war, hunger. The vivid recollection of these things sufficed him. And thus took place the first liberation of poetry from the immediate occasion, the first poetic projection of the past and distant. Our man with his individual emotion is now seen to stand among his calmer tribesmen, whom he draws into the circle of his own mood. Thus he becomes to them the seer, the inspired one, the vessel of a divine revelation. And this conception, which has never been wholly separated from the image of the poet, has been emphasized in very varying degrees at different times.

Richard Moritz Meyer, 'The Modern Poet'

Planners, builders, labourers, schemers, executives, make a city, a country, a university, habitable, give them their bones and their blood. Poets and novelists make us appreciate the life we live in them, give them their souls.

Henry S. Canby, 'Thanks to the Artists'

Come with rain, O loud Southwester!
Bring the singer, bring the nester;
Give the buried flower a dream;
Make the settled snow-bank steam;
Find the brown beneath the white;
But whate'er you do to-night,
Bathe my window, make it flow,
Melt it as the ice will go;

Melt the glass and leave the sticks
Like a hermit's crucifix;
Burst into my narrow stall;
Swing the picture on the wall;
Run the rattling pages o'er;
Scatter poems on the floor;
Turn the poet out of door.

　　　　Robert Frost, 'To the Thawing Wind'
　　　　　　　　　A Boy's Will

. . . what is meant by the word Poet? He is a
man speaking to men: a man, it is true, endowed with
a more lively sensibility, more enthusiasm and tenderness, who has a greater knowledge of human
nature, and a more comprehensive soul, than are supposed to be common among mankind; a man pleased
with his own passions and volitions, and who re-
joices more than other men in the spirit of life that is
in him; delighting to contemplate similiar volitions
and passions as manifested in the goings-on of the
universe, and habitually impelled to create them
where he does not find them.

　　　W. Wordsworth, Preface to *Lyrical Ballads*

So too I cannot understand how a Mirabeau, with
that great glowing heart, with the fire that was in it,
with the bursting tears that were in it, could not
have written verses, tragedies, poems, and touched
all hearts in that way had his course of life and education led thitherward. The grand fundamental character is that of Great Man: that the man be great.

Napoleon has words in him which are like Auster-
litz battles. Louis Fourteenth's Marshals are a kind
of poetical men withal; the things Turenne says are
full of sagacity and geniality, like the sayings of
Samuel Johnson. The great heart, the clear deep-
seeing eyes: there it lies; no man whatever, in what
province soever, can prosper at all without these.

> Thomas Carlyle, 'The Hero as Poet'
> *On Heroes, Hero-Worship, and the*
> *Heroic in History*

And thus, in full, there are four classes: the men
who feel nothing, and therefore see truly; the men
who feel strongly, think weakly, and see untruly
(second order of poets); the men who feel strongly,
think strongly, and see truly (first order of poets);
and the men who, strong as human creatures can be,
are yet submitted to influences stronger than they,
and see in a sort untruly, because what they see is
inconceivably above them. This last is the usual condition of prophetic inspiration.

> John Ruskin, 'Of the Pathetic Fallacy'
> *Modern Painters*

One more royal trait properly belongs to the poet.
I mean his cheerfulness, without which no man can
be a poet,—for beauty is his aim. He loves virtue, not
for its obligations, but for its grace: he delights in the
world, in man, in woman, for the lovely light that
sparkles from them. Beauty, the spirit of joy and
hilarity, he sheds over the universe. And the true

bards have been noted for their firm and cheerful temper. Homer lies in sunshine; Chaucer is glad and erect . . . not less sovereign and cheerful—much more sovereign and cheerful, is the tone of Shakespeare. His name suggests joy and emancipation to the heart of men. If he should appear in any company of human souls, who would not march in his troop?

R. W. Emerson, 'Shakespeare', *Representative Men*

> Into the middle of my thought I crept
> And on the bosom of the angel lay,
> Lived all my life at once; and oh I wept
> My own future to be.

Stanley Kunitz, 'The Words of the Preacher'
Intellectual Things

Perhaps only the poet knows how close he comes sometimes to the boundaries of that other country where self is lost in the stored memories of the race, intelligence in instinct, and humanity in a great animal kinship. He is often amazed by his own intuitive flashes, but not too much amazed, if he is a true artist, to get them down on paper in some sort of intelligible order. If he can convey to his readers the sense of mysterious origin with which the suggestion endowed his mind, then he has succeeded. Someone has whispered in his ear, perhaps not in words, but rather in a series of bright visions like an unfolding dream. He must make these visions materialize in words, and he must get them down with the dew of his astonishment still on them. We recognize the results of such moments wherever we find them, whether Blake is telling us of the lion's ruddy eyes that flowed with tears of gold, or staid New England Emerson suddenly intones: 'Daughters of Time, the hypocritic Days, muffled and drab like solemn dervishes. . . .'

> Jessica Nelson North, 'Quality in Madness'

I had not taken the first step in knowledge;
I had not learned to let go with the hands,
As still I have not learned to with the heart,
And have no wish to with the heart—nor need,
That I can see. The mind—is not the heart.
I may yet live, as I know others live,
To wish in vain to let go with the mind—
Of cares, at night, to sleep; but nothing tells me
That I need learn to let go with the heart.

> Robert Frost, 'Wild Grapes', *New Hampshire*

Nothing worth speaking of happened . . . I took down some thin paper and wrote on it a little poem called St. Agnes' Eve.

> John Keats, *Letters*

Cries the poet every day:
Ego, mei, mihi, me!

> Christopher Morley, *Inward Ho!*

Alfred (Tennyson) is always carrying a bit of chaos around with him, and turning it into cosmos.

> Thomas Carlyle

Great things happen: sometimes in a burst of instantaneous completion; oftenertimes by slow indignations, through every grade of postponement, doubtful addition, and nail-paring disgust. But they do happen, and sooner or later the man with a blessing hears about them.

Christopher Morley, 'Jamie Comes to Hy-Brasil'
Romany Stain

But the sentient, the living, the laughing, the
    grieving—
The wild snorting poets that scour the plains
And lave in the ocean of boundless emotion
Think life is a dungeon, and howl in their chains.

John Jay Chapman, 'Souls in Prison'

At length, starting to his feet (it was now winter and very cold) Orlando swore one of the most remarkable oaths of his lifetime, for it bound him to a servitude than which none is stricter. 'I'll be blasted,' he said, 'if I ever write another word, or try to write another word, to please Nick Greene or the Muse. Bad, good, or indifferent, I'll write, from this day forward, to please myself,' and here he made as if he were tearing a whole budget of papers across and tossing them in the face of that sneering loose-lipped man.   Virginia Woolf, *Orlando*

Imagination changes the scale of everything, and makes a thousand patterns of the woof of nature, without disturbing a single thread. Or rather—since

it is nature itself that imagines—it turns to music
what was only a strain; as if the universal vibration,
suddenly ashamed of having been so long silent and
useless, had burst into tears and laughter at its own
folly, and in so doing had become wise.

George Santayana, *Soliloquies in England*

People made of skin and bone are just as incredible
as people made of ink and paper; the Almighty allows Himself a much more frantic latitude in invent-
ing people than we writers do. . . . Really to write
about people, one must contrive to be present at a
scene that—in flesh and blood—one never succeeds
in witnessing; one must contrive to know people
when they are alone. And I am sure that when people
are alone they are entirely incredible.

Stella Benson, *Pull Devil, Pull Baker*

The faint conceptions I have of poems to come
bring the blood frequently into my forehead.

John Keats, *Letters*

At times, I have got drunk on brimming eyes;
Wrestled alone with him who comes by night,
And with a drop of scalding oil have lost him:
At times, fused night with day in fervent thinking
Till the skull sweated . . .
Richard Hughes, 'Travel-Piece', *Confessio Juvenis*

If there is a famine of invention in the land, like
Joseph's brethren we must travel far for food; we
must visit the remote and rich ancients; but an in-

ventive genius may safely stay at home; that like the
widow's cruse, is divinely replenished from within;
and affords us a miraculous delight.

Edward Young,
'Conjectures on Original Composition'

Milton's purity is more eager. In the most exciting
parts of Wordsworth you always feel, you never
forget, that what you have before you is the excitement of a recluse. There is nothing of the stir of life;
nothing of the brawl of the world. But Milton,
though always a scholar by trade, though solitary
in old age, was through life intent on great affairs,
lived close to great scenes, watched a revolution, and
if not an actor in it, was at least secretary to the
actors.

Walter Bagehot,
'Wordsworth, Tennyson and Browning,
or Pure, Ornate and Grotesque Art in
English Poetry'

Nobody else I ever knew has given me such a sense
of having freedom, a margin of actual self-deter-
mination. . . . Firmness in refusal to comply with
external forces except when his internal force is in
accord, is the trait that I am most frequently aston-
ished by in him. . . . He left Dartmouth, not because he didn't like hard work, nor because he was
restless, but because he found college a mill for
being made into 'decent boards', and he was going to
stay a growing tree. . . . No real experience comes,
he thinks, when you can take the sting out of it by

telling yourself you can use it in a book or otherwise. The experiences that toughen your character or furnish your mind are experiences you are submerged in. . . . He is not 'a decent product of life's ironing-out.' He is an original man whose extraordinariness is partly due to his never having bargained away any of the endowments of the genus man.

Sidney Cox, *Robert Frost*

He had been, in fact, one of those rare critical intelligences, possessed of a natural aptitude for what is best and most hopeful among their contemporaries' work—such men as, amid the hurly-burly of contemporary enthusiasm and disdain, have an instinctive leaning toward the few, usually depressed and neglected, figures who will afterwards seem to be the giants of the age in which they lived. He had enjoyed *a sense of his own age*, had recognized its pattern while the pattern was yet incomplete, and—because it is only our misapprehension of the present which prevents our looking into the immediate future, our ignorance of today and of its real import as apart from its spurious tendencies and requirements—had anticipated many problems, both on the esthetic and on the moral plane, in which the fate of modern poetry is still concerned.

Peter Quennell, *Baudelaire and the Symbolists*

I may say of him here, that he is the only person I ever knew who answered to the idea of the man of genius. He is the only person from whom I ever learnt anything. He was the first poet I ever knew. His genius at that time had angelic wings and fed on manna. He talked on forever; his thoughts did not seem to come with labour and effort; but as if borne on the gusts of genius, and as if the wings of his imagination lifted him from off his feet. His voice rolled on the ear like the pealing organ, and its sound alone was the music of thought. His mind was clothed with wings; and raised on them, he lifted philosophy to heaven. In his descriptions, you then saw the progress of human happiness and liberty in bright and never-ending succession, like the steps of Jacob's ladder, with airy shapes ascending and descending, and with the voice of God at the top of the ladder.

William Hazlitt, 'Coleridge'

I think continually of those who were truly great.
Who, from the womb, remembered the soul's history
Through corridors of light where the hours are suns
Endless and singing. Whose lovely ambition
Was that their lips, still touched with fire,
Should tell of the Spirit clothed from head to foot in
    song.
And who hoarded from the Spring branches
The desires falling across their bodies like blossoms.

What is precious is never to forget
The essential delight of the blood drawn from age-
    less springs

Breaking through rocks in worlds before our earth.
Never to deny its pleasure in the morning simple
   light
Nor its grave evening demand for love.
Never to allow gradually the traffic to smother
With noise and fog the flowering of the spirit.

Near the snow, near the sun, in the highest fields
See how these names are fêted by the waving grass
And by the streamers of white cloud
And whispers of wind in the listening sky.

The names of those who in their lives fought for life
Who wore at their hearts the fire's centre.
Born of the sun they travelled a short while towards
   the sun,
And left the vivid air signed with their honour.

              Stephen Spender, xxx, *Poems*

   Most things are strong in one direction,—a straw
longitudinally, a board in the direction of its edge,
a knee transversely to the grain—but the brave man
is a perfect sphere, which cannot fall on its flat side,
and is equally strong every day.

              H. D. Thoreau, *Journals*

   Man is perishable. That may be; but let us perish
resisting, and if it is only nothingness that awaits us,
let us act so that it will be an injustice.

              Etienne de Senancour, *Obermann*

Whatever the poets pretend, it is plain they give immortality to none but themselves; 'tis Homer and Vergil we reverence and admire, not Achilles or Aeneas.   Jonathan Swift, 'Thoughts'

> . . . and grant
> That I myself for portions of the year
> May handle nothing and set eyes on nothing
> But what the great and passionate have used
> Throughout so many varying centuries
> We take it for the norm.
>
> William Butler Yeats,
> 'A Prayer on Going Into My House'
> *The Wild Swans at Coole*

Our house must be honest and solid like our work. Everything we buy must be the same. Everything we wear, even. I can't stand anything false. Everything must ring like Elizabethan English and like those gentlemen I always seem to be mentioning, 'the Poets'. There is a light upon them, especially upon the Elizabethans and our 'special' set—Keats, Wordsworth, Coleridge, Shelley, De Quincey, and Co., which I feel is like the bright star shining which must hang in the sky above Heron as we drive home. Those are the people with whom I want to live, those are the men I feel are our brothers, and the queer thing is that I feel there is a great golden loop linking them to Shakespeare's time.

Katherine Mansfield, *Letters*

I know what wages beauty gives,
How hard a life her servant lives,
Yet praise the winters gone:
There is not a fool can call me friend,
And I may dine at journey's end
With Landor and with Donne.
William Butler Yeats, 'To a Young Beauty'
The Wild Swans at Coole

We carry with us all the wonders we seek without
us: there is all Africa and her prodigies in us; we are
that bold and adventurous piece of Nature, which he
that studies wisely learns in a compendium what
others labour at in a divided piece and endless volume. Sir Thomas Browne, *Religio Medici*

With a heart of furious fancies
Whereof I am commander,
With a burning spear,
And a horse of air,
To the wilderness I wander;

With a knight of ghosts and shadows,
I summoned am to tourney:
Ten leagues beyond
The wide world's end;
Methinks it is no journey.
'Tom o' Bedlam', *Giles Earle, His Book*, 1615

I see Every thing I paint in this World, but Everybody does not see alike. To the Eyes of a Miser a

Guinea is far more beautiful than the Sun, & a bag
worn with the use of Money has more beautiful proportions than a Vine filled with Grapes. The tree
which moves some to tears of Joy is in the Eyes of
others only a Green thing which stands in the way.
Some see Nature all Ridicule and Deformity, & by
these I shall not regulate my proportions; & some
scarce see Nature at all. But to the eyes of the Man of
Imagination, Nature is Imagination itself. As a man is,
so he sees.

William Blake, *Letters*

They would not find me changed from him they
 knew—
Only more sure of all I thought was true.

Robert Frost, 'Into My Own', *A Boy's Will*

The only strength for me is to be found in the
sense of a personal presence everywhere, it scarcely
matters whether it be called human or divine; a presence which only makes itself felt at first in this and
that particular form and feature. Into this presence
we come, not by leaving behind what are usually
called earthly things, or by loving them less, but by
living more intensely in them; for it is literally true
that this world *is* everything to us, if only we choose
to make it so, if only we 'live in the present' *because*
it is eternity.

R. L. Nettleship, *Letters*

I thank God, and with joy I mention it, I was never afraid of Hell, nor never grew pale at the description of that place.

Sir Thomas Browne, *Religio Medici*

If a person liked anything, if he took snuff heartily, it was sufficient. He would understand, by analogy, the pungency of other things beside Irish blackguard or Scotch rapee.

William Hazlitt,
'On The Conversation Of Authors'

I have heard what the talkers were talking, the talk
 of the beginning and the end,
But I do not talk of the beginning or the end.

There was never any more inception than there is
 now,
Nor any more youth or age than there is now,
And will never be any more perfection than there is
 now,
Nor any more heaven or hell than there is now.

Walt Whitman, 'Song of Myself', *Leaves of Grass*

Perhaps none of the poems is more purely and typically Shellian than 'The Cloud', and it is interesting to note how essentially it springs from the faculty of make-believe. The same thing is conspicuous, throughout his singing; it is the child's faculty of make-believe raised to the nth power. He is still at play, save only that his play is such as manhood stops to watch, and his playthings are those which the gods give their children. The universe is his box of toys. He dabbles his fingers in the day-fall. He is gold-dusty with tumbling amidst the stars. He makes bright mischief with the moon. The meteors nuzzle their noses in his hand. He teases into growling the kennelled thunder, and laughs at the shaking of its fiery chain. He dances in and out of the gates of heaven: its floor is littered with his broken fancies. He runs wild over the fields of ether. He chases the rolling world. He gets between the feet of the horses of the sun. He stands in the lap of patient Nature and twines her loosened tresses after a hundred wilful patterns to see how she will look nicest in his song.

Francis Thompson, *Shelley*

While always holding fast to his own personality, a personality so strong that he could not have concealed it even if he had wanted to, yet to each one of his friends Keats turns a different side. To Bailey, he philosophizes and opens up the heart of his spiritual puzzles; to Haydon, he chats about art, gossips of mutual friends, and falls in, as far as may be, with what he knows Haydon to be preoccupied with at the time; to Reynolds, he talks pure poetry, and often merely wanders on after the thread of his wandering fancies, certain that Reynolds will understand; to his brother he is everything by turns, but always in a taken-for-granted sort of way, quite unlike his attitude toward anyone else.

Amy Lowell, *John Keats*

God keep me from ever completing anything. This whole book is but a draught—nay, but the draught of a draught. Oh, Time, Strength, Cash and Patience!   Herman Melville, *Moby Dick*

Give me Chaucer in preference. He slaps us on the shoulder, and makes us spring up while the dew is on the grass, and while the long shadows play about it in all quarters. We feel strong with the freshness round us, and we return with a keened appetite, having such a companion in our walk.

W. S. Landor, *Imaginary Conversations*

All beauty comes from beautiful blood and a beautiful brain.

Walt Whitman, Preface to *Leaves of Grass*, 1855

I can see no reason why man will not presently give up all major beliefs, and simply surrender himself to what is perhaps the first principle of his own present state as a conscious creature—an insatiable curiosity.

Conrad Aiken, 'What I Believe'

It is not that poets are lonely. They are alone in the countries of the mind when they go there to get their poems and bring them back. They would allow no company there, and what they do there may be guessed by the more ingeniously inventive critics. But their speculations will be in error if they prove the poet unhappy in his solitary journey. And the

poet would not ordinarily be lonely in this world's
company, except that he sees too clearly the webs
and veils, the nakedness and its poor disguise, that
complicates ordinary acquaintance. Who ever knows
another human being? The poet, naturally a warm
and friendly sort, agonizes over the silences, the de-
lays, the awkward aims of his personal relationships.
A friend said of Henry James, 'In spite of admiration and curiosity I left our meetings entirely to
chance, for I soon discovered two daunting facts
about him. Firstly, that he was easily bored (not
merely in an ordinary but in an excruciating sense
of the word), and secondly, that he minded intensely the dislocations and disappointments which are
inevitable in all human relations. They made him
groan and writhe and worry. The measure of how
much he minded them could be read in the fre-
quency, extravagance, and emphasis of signals that
all was really well, across even those small rifts (to
him they had the horror of gulfs) which absence and
accident open up between people.'

John Holmes, 'Nothing is Lost'

We live in a web of associated memories; our general map—the chart thanks to which we know more
or less clearly where we put what, recognize analogies, form classes, make order out of chaos and ac-
cumulate experience—is a network of memories. And
one of ourselves, the loudest voiced one, the one we
usually think of when we say I, corresponds to the
spot on that map where the most frequent and fa-

miliar memories cross each other, as the railroads of
a country cross at its capital.

                    H. B. Brewster, *The Prison*

    A great poet, who appears in illiterate times, ab-
sorbs into his sphere all the light which is anywhere
radiating. Every intellectual jewel, every flower of
sentiment, it is his fine office to bring to his people;
and he comes to value his memory equally with his
invention.

R. W. Emerson, 'Shakespeare', *Representative Men*

    . . . man was to be treated as a musical instrument,
and if any viol was to be made of sound timber and
kept well tuned always, it was he, so that when the
bow of events is drawn across him he may vibrate
and resound in perfect harmony. A sensitive soul
will be continually trying its strings to see if they
are in tune. A man's body must be rasped down
exactly to a shaving. It is of far more importance
than the wood of a Cremona violin.

                    H. D. Thoreau, *Journals*

    I hope I have some range in the appreciation of
Beauty. I can see it all the way from exquisite
through homely and mean, even to vile.

             Robert Frost, *from notes on a lecture*

    Upon wild plains omnipotent
    A conquering quality Danger was.
    You saw it always imminent,

A sly shadow on the grass.
It was an agent in the air,
Active as sunshine, yielding health
And Death, but not Death everywhere.

Welborn Hope, 'Danger'

There are moments when Dickens is possessed by
the power of writing: he is carried away. That is
bliss. It certainly is not shared by writers today. The
death of Cheedle: dawn falling upon the edge of
night. One realizes exactly the mood of the writer
and how he wrote, as it were, for himself, but it was
not his will. He *was* the falling dawn, and he *was*
the physician going to Bar.

Katherine Mansfield, *Journals*

If a sparrow comes before my window, I take part
in its existence and pick about the gravel.

John Keats, *Letters*

I do not ask the wounded person how he feels—I
myself become the wounded person.

Walt Whitman, 'Song of Myself', *Leaves of Grass*

Not I, not I, but the wind that blows through me!
A fine wind is blowing the new direction of Time.
If only I let it bear me, carry me, if only it carry me!
If only I am sensitive, subtle, oh, delicate, a winged
    gift!
If only, most lovely of all, I yield myself and am
    borrowed

By the fine fine wind that takes its course through
    the chaos of the world
Like a fine, an exquisite chisel, a wedge-blade in-
    serted;
If only I am keen and hard like the sheer tip of a
    wedge
Driven by invisible blows,
The rock shall split, we shall come to wonder, we
    shall find the Hesperides.
Oh, for the wonder that bubbles into my soul,
I would be a good fountain, a good well-head,
Would blur no whisper, spoil no expression.

D. H. Lawrence,
'Song of a Man Who Has Come Through'
Look! We Have Come Through

He gloried in the strong sensory-stimulus of glowing colour, of dazzling light; in the more complex
motory-stimulus of intricate, abrupt and plastic
form. . . . He delighted in the angular, indented,
intertwining, labyrinthine varieties of line and surface which call for the most delicate and at the same
time the most agile, adjustments of the eye. He
caught at the edges of things. . . . Spikes and wedges
and swords run riot in his work. . . . He loved the
grinding, clashing and rending sibilants and explo-
sives as Tennyson the tender-hefted liquids.

C. H. Herford

Of Hopkins' imagery, there is not much in general
to be said, but that 'not much' is all. He had that
acute and sharp sensuous awareness essential to all

great poets. He was physically aware of textures, surfaces, colors, patterns of every kind; aware acutely of the earth's diurnal course, of growth and decay, of animality in man and of vitality in all things. Everywhere there is passionate apprehension, passionate expression and equally that passion for form without which these other passions are spendthrift. But the form is inherent in the passion. For, as Emerson remarked with his occasional deep insight, 'It is not metres, but a metre-making argument, that makes a poem—a thought so passionate and alive, that, like the spirit of a plant or an animal, it has an architecture of its own, and adorns nature with a new thing.'

Herbert Read, *Form in Modern Poetry*

It matters not where or how far you travel—the farther commonly the worse—but how much alive you are. All that a man has to say or do that can possibly concern mankind, is in some shape or other to tell the story of his love—to sing, and if he is fortunate and keeps alive, he will be forever in love.

H. D. Thoreau, *Journals*

As our blood labours to beget
Spirits, as like souls as it can,
Because such fingers need to knit
That subtile knot, which makes us man:
So must pure lovers souls descend
To affections and to faculties,
Which sense may reach and apprehend,
Else a great Prince in prison lies.

John Donne, 'The Ecstasy'

It isn't the money that makes people start writing, and stick to it; it is the hope of publication. In its highest phase the writing mania proceeds the wish to break down, somehow, the awful barrier which exists between soul and soul, and share even bitterness, if there is neither knowledge nor joy to be shared; in its lower manifestations it may be merely exhibitionism, and yet, there too, is the wistful hope of being better understood.

Don Marquis

And cared it into song—strict care, strict joy!
Caring for grief he cared his grief away:
And those sad songs, tho' woe be all the theme,
Do not make us grieve who read them now
Because the poet makes grief beautiful.

James Stephens, *Strict Joy*

But what are you going to do about people when you're not with them? Into what faraway loneliness do their minds travel? What uncanny thoughts do they think? You can visualize them, see them walking, laughing, sulking; see their amusing clothes (so remarkably a part of themselves), the delicate way their hair grows, their bright serious eyes; hear their unmistakable voices repeating favorite opinions. Does all that go on, just the same, and you not there? Yes, they are pursuing their own relentless privacies, but are they real? Even if they were dead, would they be any farther away? You grope clumsily toward them, but is it really they you seek, or some

new reassurance of yourself? . . . The phantoms
of so many friends rise before you. What's happen-
ing to them? Tell me, tell me everything (you'd
like to say): I'll never hold it against you. I'll match
each grief that plagues you with grievances of my
own. Ring, telephone; come, letter; I need you.

Christopher Morley, *Human Being*

A great and available reserve of sheer intensity—
intensity of perception and emotion—it is in his pos-
session of this that a great artist differs most deeply
from his fellows. In no vague or rhetorical sense of
the words, he sees and hears more intensely.

C. E. Montague, 'The Last Question of All'
A Writer's Notes on His Trade

I have a hunger food is gall to—
It starves more sweetly on the thought
Of that light thing I could but call to,
That glimmering image scarcely caught.

George Dillon, 'The Mad Hunter'
The Flowering Stone

Poor human nature, so richly endowed with nerves
of anguish, so splendidly organized for pain and
sorrow, is but slenderly equipped for joy. . . . A
sense of ineffable joy, attainable at will, and equal
in intensity and duration to (let us say) an attack
of sciatica, would go far to equalize the one-sided
conditions under which we live.

George du Maurier, *Peter Ibbetson*

In good health, the air is a cordial of incredible virtue. Crossing a bare common, in snow puddles, at twilight, under a clouded sky, without having in my thoughts any occurrence of special good fortune, I have enjoyed a perfect exhilaration. I am glad to the brink of fear.

    R. W. Emerson, 'Nature', *The Conduct of Life*

Snow falling and night falling fast oh fast
In a field I looked into going past,
And the ground almost covered smooth in snow,
But a few weeds and stubble showing last.

The woods around it have it—it is theirs.
All animals are smothered in their lairs.
I am too absent-spirited to count;
Their loneliness includes me unawares.

And lonely as it is that loneliness
Will be more lonely ere it will be less—
A blanker whiteness of benighted snow
With no expression, nothing to express.

They cannot scare me with their empty spaces
Between stars—on stars where no human race is.
I have it in me so much nearer home
To scare myself with my own desert places.
    Robert Frost, 'Desert Places', *A Further Range*

To be normal is to be a standard, but not, as things are and are likely to remain, an average; and to inquire into the characters of the norm or to ask who

are normal is to raise a question as to value. The artist departs from the average, but so do other people.
His departure, however, is one of the reasons why
we attend to his work; other people's departures
may be reasons why we should not. If the artist's
organism is such as to allow him a fuller life than the
average, with less unnecessary interference between
its component impulses, then plainly we should do
well to be more like him, if we can and as far as we
can.   I. A. Richards, 'The Normality of the Artist'
                        Principles of Literary Criticism

Emily Dickinson had a genius for trifles, peculiar
to herself—in her poetry she was always proving the
importance of the homely, the neglected detail, as
if it were her chief business on earth. She was high-
strung—life, every morsel of it, was momentous.
And so, when she wrote to friends, she conveyed a
breathless attitude. Her wit loved the material at
hand.   Anonymous

> Man with his burning soul
> Has but an hour of breath
> To build a ship of truth
> In which his soul may sail—
> Sail on the sea of death
> For death takes toll
> Of beauty, courage, youth,
> All but truth.
>   John Masefield, 'Truth'
>   *The Widow in the Bye Street*

There are people who appear to think only with the brain, or with whatever may be the specific thinking organ; while others think with all the body and all the soul, with the blood, with the marrow of the bones, with the heart, with the belly, with the lungs, with the life.

Miguel de Unamuno, *The Tragic Sense of Life*

I hate people who meet Time half-way. I am for no compromise with that inevitable spoiler.

Charles Lamb, 'My Relations', *Last Essays of Elia*

At first I shouted: 'God,' I cried,
'My valuable dream has died!'
He did not even look aside,
So I went nearer. 'God,' I said,
'I suppose you know my dream is dead.'

Roberta Teale Swartz, 'Preoccupation'
Liliput

Today I am hardening my heart. I am walking all around my heart and building up the defences. I do not mean to leave a loophole even for a tuft of violets to grow in. Give me a hard heart, O Lord! Lord, harden thou my heart!

Katherine Mansfield, *Journals*

I have relapsed into those abstractions which are my only life. I feel escaped from a new strange and threatening sorrow, and am thankful for it. There is an awful warmth about my heart like a load of immortality.

John Keats, *Letters*

INDEX OF AUTHORS

INDEX OF AUTHORS

INDEX OF AUTHORS